NEW RESTAURANT
INTERIOR DESIGN

DINNER TIME

FLAMANT 11

DINNER TIME

NEW RESTAURANT
INTERIOR DESIGN

Copyright © 2019 English language edition by
Flamant for sale in Europe and America.
Flamant is an imprint of:
Hoaki Books, S.L.
C/ Ausiàs March 128.
08013 Barcelona, Spain
Phone: 0034 93 595 22 83
Fax: 0034 93 265 48 83
info@hoakibooks.com
www.hoaki.com

Copyright © 2019 by Sandu Publishing Co., Ltd.
Sponsored by Design 360°
– Concept and Design Magazine
Edited and produced by
Sandu Publishing Co., Ltd.
www.sandupublishing.com

Executive Editor: Krystle Zhang
Design Director: Wang Shaoqiang
Cover & Book Designer: Wu Yanting

Cover photos by Infinity Mind

ISBN: 978-84-17084-11-0
D.L.: B 13437-2019

Printed in China

CONTENTS

PREFACE

Greg Bleier
Studio UNLTD

We all have stories of the magic of a well-designed restaurant space. When done right, the eating environment can play a key role in creating major moments in people's lives. You recall a meal with friends or family in a place where the mood was perfect and the food delightful. It could be a favorite neighborhood restaurant from years past, or it might be that wonderful jewel where you and your loved ones brought in the New Year.

These experiences seem to matter more and more. As the global economy grows and we see more of an emphasis on working hard, cooking less, and enjoying the spoils of exciting culinary options, the restaurant space becomes a very important component in the restaurant owner's conceptual vision. In its most simplistic terms, eating out is about the food itself and the company you bring, but a well-designed space delivers something that is much more compelling, complex, and rewarding.

Restaurant interiors, like all other creative ventures, reflect the moment and trends. But one trend that is truly exciting is that design is becoming more of a factor in the restaurant industry: the humblest of establishments now place emphasis on it. The approach we take at my studio is that no food and beverage establishment is too small or insignificant to afford or require good design. Whether it be a small taco stand, a fast-casual noodles shop, or a formal seafood restaurant, even the smallest interactions throughout the day create moments that live on within each and every one of us.

More interestingly still, operators of some of the top restaurants are taking more design risks and embracing a casual dining environment. Stuffy dining rooms are being left in the past. They either survive as kitschy relics of a bygone era or have simply disappeared as patrons have gravitated towards energetic and engaging dining experiences. Despite the disappearance of the white-tablecloth restaurant, the seriousness of the cuisine has not been sacrificed. In fact, the business of delivering quality food in all areas of the restaurant industry is becoming the norm more and more. Savvy consumers move away from fast-food options knowing that they can do better for themselves and the planet. And dining rooms have become more open and louder, with much of the kitchen now exposed. The mystique of the making has gone, creating a stronger connection between chef, operator, and guest.

Since I am discussing trends, I would be remiss if I did not mention how in this digital age we crave uniqueness and special touches to enrich and enliven our busy lives. The role of experiences shared through social media such as Instagram has very much planted its flag in the industry, providing an interactive quality as well as publicity for establishments. Although more and more clients look for that "Instagram moment," my studio takes the approach that those moments will come organically when a well-designed project is delivered.

Getting a client's message across—for example, telling the story of the brand or the chef—is at the forefront of what we do at my studio. Creating a story that connects with people is the key ingredient in creating a good restaurant design. From the moment when guests arrive in a space, they should not be confused; the initial message should be strong, and the design details should unfold throughout the experience. There needs to be a symbiotic relationship between atmosphere, branding, service, food, and beverages. Every part of the atmosphere must be considered, from music to the things you touch, such as tableware and napkins. Everything must work together like a grand symphony. It's important to deeply understand the vision of the client to execute this on the highest level. We immerse ourselves in learning about what the client is trying to communicate. We then use our skillset to interpret that information as a design concept that supports the vision.

We find that it's critical to take ego out of the equation and embrace the learning process and the journey of discovery that we take alongside the client. While what we do as designers is very important to the overall result, it is not the most important element of the overall project. Successfully creating an iconic restaurant with staying power is very much a team effort. It must never be forgotten that the restaurant business is one of the most difficult industries in which to find success.

Most restaurants do not last a single year. Our clients are entrusting us as designers to deliver the best product we can, and they often have everything on the line. The funding may come from their life savings, or it may come from an investment fund, but either way, the decisions involved in designing a restaurant should never be taken lightly, as they often have quite significant consequences.

Le Corbusier referred to a house as a "machine for living in." I like to refer to a restaurant as a machine for working in. In the case of commercial design, I would argue that food and beverage establishments, above all others, require a lot of attention to be paid to a variety of components. It's not just about the guest experience. You must consider the people who will be working there: put yourself in the shoes of the bartenders, servers, hosts, cooks, and managers. You could design the most aesthetically pleasing restaurant, but if the machine doesn't work and tasks can't be performed efficiently, then the client has been done a disservice and the restaurant may unjustly struggle.

Dinner Time takes us on a journey to the latest in remarkable design efforts from multiple cultures around the globe. In it you will find some of the most thoughtful and engaging projects of the last few years—projects that celebrate the incredible diversity within the global culinary community. It delivers a compelling story of restaurant design that reveals current trends and how some of the most talented creatives on the planet have developed and interpreted them. And it's fascinating to see the juxtaposition of stark, graphic, early-eighties influences with softer, organic, Bohemian, late-seventies-inspired spaces or with highly technical contemporary designs.

Dinner Time arouses the senses in the same way as a perfectly executed restaurant concept would. Enjoy the exploration, and bon appétit!

Creating a story that connects with people is the key ingredient in creating a good restaurant design. From the moment when guests arrive in a space, they should not be confused; the initial message should be strong, and the design details should unfold throughout the experience. There needs to be a symbiotic relationship between atmosphere, branding, service, food, and beverages.

HINOAK

Area: **130 m²**
Location: **Melbourne, Australia**

Craft, harmony and a delicate balance between built form and natural material underpin the design for Hinoak, a modern but authentic interpretation of the traditional Korean barbecue in Melbourne's south-east. The studio was commissioned for the project's interiors and branding, inspired by traditional Chinese iconography.

The concept for the project took design cues from the elegant work of Japanese architect Kengo Kuma, exploring the relationship between humanity, nature and design. The result is an interior that is warm, cosy and intimate, filled with the intriguing play of light that filters through the slatted exterior. The branding for the restaurant focused on the Chinese symbol for 'fire'— commonly used in Korean culture, this character has been cut into the external battening, recalling Korea's fine craft traditions.

Design Agency: **Biasol**
Photography: **James Morgan**
Materials: **Blackbutt Timber, Victorian Ash Timber, Concrete Rendered Wall, Terrazzo Tile, Fibonacci Stone FIB-299-P12-Honed, Lime Washed Existing Timber Floor**

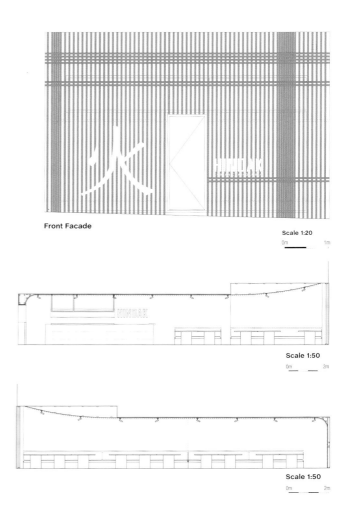

Front Facade

Scale 1:20
0m ___ 1m

Scale 1:50
0m ___ 2m

Scale 1:50
0m ___ 2m

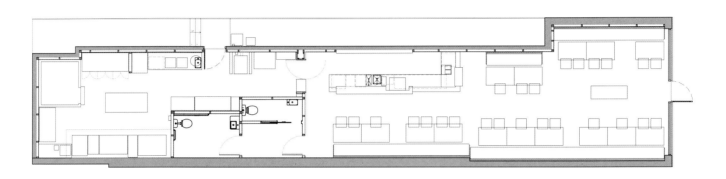

THE BUDAPEST CAFÉ

Area: **178 m²**
Location: **Chengdu, China**

Filmmaker Wes Anderson's distinctive visual style provided the inspiration for The Budapest Café in Chengdu, China. The design draws on Anderson's meticulous, memorable and magical worlds to create an inviting destination with whimsical character and international appeal. The Budapest Café is designed to offer an experience that detaches patrons from the hustle and bustle of everyday life. The client specifically engaged an Australian design practice to create an international hospitality experience, and requested a space that would appeal to social media-savvy females who enjoy café culture. The result demonstrates Biasol's international capabilities fused with the local design style.

The modern, minimalist and refreshing interpretation is defined by design, materiality and brand. The building façade projects a sense of grandeur with an arch framing the entrance and welcoming patrons to The Budapest Café. Once inside, customers are invited to engage with the physical design of the café, much like a stage set for patrons to play out their own story. The concept, colors and details continue through the branding, which is integrated into the design of the café to contribute to the imaginative and evocative space.

Design Agency: **Biasol**
Photography: **James Morgan**
Materials: **Signorino—Terrazzo, Artedomus—Marble**

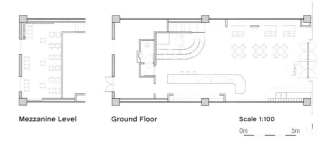

Mezzanine Level   Ground Floor   Scale 1:100

0m   5m

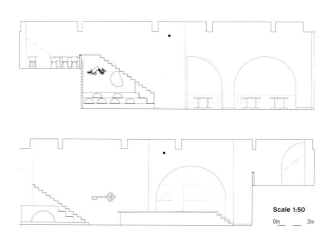

Scale 1:50

0m   2m

NO. 19

Area: **190 m²**
Location: **Melbourne, Australia**

Following the success of their first café—St Rose in Essendon—husband-and-wife team Domenic and Diana Caruso secured a new Ascot Vale site, approximately five kilometres north-west of Melbourne's CBD. Their vision was for a sophisticated but welcoming venue that would set a new standard for casual dining—a dynamic addition to Melbourne's much-loved café culture.

Spanning both interiors and branding, the concept was an elegant, timeless space inspired by the Greek delicatessens that flourished around Melbourne in the 1950s. Located in a busy shopping strip, the site offered a promising starting point—4.5-metre ceilings, skylights that flood the space with natural light, and a deep rectangular footprint. A key priority in this project was to develop a strong relationship between the interior design and the brand itself. Every element—from the menus and coasters to the deli paper and crockery—has been carefully conceived, reflecting Biasol's integrated approach.

Design Agency: **Biasol**
Photography: **Ari Hatzis**
Materials: **Concrete, Hexagonal Tiles, Pale Timber, Brass, Felt / Velvet / Houndstooth Fabric, Resin Flooring, Tiento Tiles— Popham Long Demi Hex Tiles col. Turquoise/Pistachio**

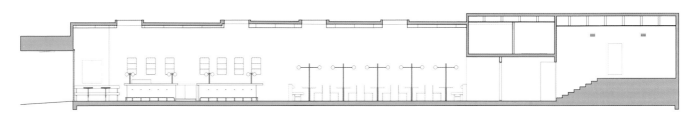

Scale 1:100

0m   5m

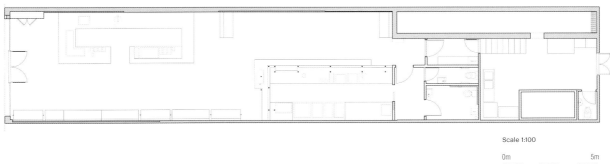

Scale 1:100

0m   5m

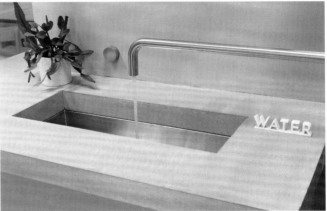

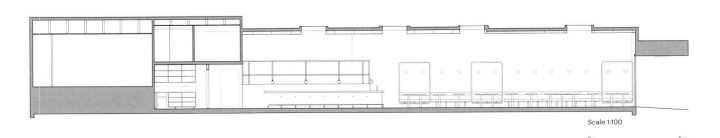

Scale 1:100

0m   5m

PIRAÑA

Area: **130 m²**
Location: **London, England**

With bold colour combinations to catch the eye, Piraña's exterior features mosaics of blue and white tile and striking window façades dominated by a red metal framework. Inside, a rich, sensory colour and material palette creates a playful, trend-agnostic aesthetic. Apart from the chairs and lights, Sella Concept custom-designed every fixture and item of furniture—including the booths, bar, banquette, tables, stools, floors and bathroom sinks. Some of their most attention-grabbing features include the bespoke floor in jade terrazzo and micro mosaic tiling at the bar, with earthy red upholstery and curved timber slats to tie the space together.

Interior Design: **Sella Concept**
Photography: **Nicholas Worley**
Client: **Brothers, Alastair and Nicholas Heathcote**
Materials: **Tibor & Kvadrat—RAF Simons (Fabric), Servomuto (Lighting), Vintage Chairs, Micro Mosaico (Bar Tiles), Terrazzo by Huguet (Floor & Bespoke Sink)**

PENTOLINA

Area: **122 m²**
Location: **Melbourne, Australia**

Pentolina is a new Italian casual dining restaurant, bringing the art of traditional pasta making found in Rome's winding laneways to Little Collins Street in Melbourne. Designed by Biasol, it captures Italy's passion for food, design and good company, fusing it with Melbourne's hospitality aesthetic. A double-curved marble counter evokes the nostalgia of old-school pasta bars and unifies the key functions of the restaurant, while bringing guests together to engage with each other and staff. The material and colour palette captures the European character of Rome and Melbourne, with hand-rendered concrete walls, rose-coloured marble, terrazzo flooring and grooved Tasmanian oak.

Design Agency: **Biasol**
Photography: **Jack Lovel**
Materials: **Signorino—Terrazzo Montecarlo (Floor), Signorino—Karaman Marble (Bar), Dulux Red Marble, Dulux Powdercoat, Medium Bronze / Satin Black, Dulux Blackboard Paint, Tasmanian Oak Timber Cladding & Table Tops, Instyle—Upholstery**

Scale 1:100
0m   5m

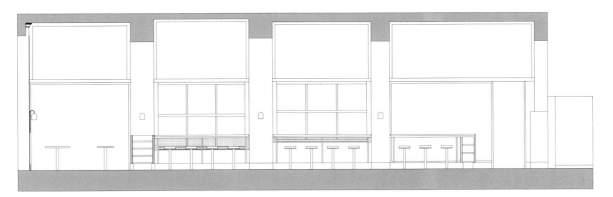

BURRITO LOCO

Area: **70 m²**
Location: **Prague, Czech Republic**

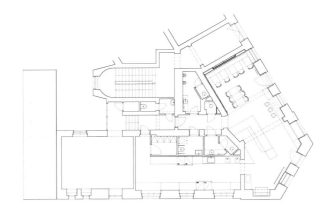

Mexico is full of colours. A distinctive feature is variety and glamour. The architects from studio Formafatal have kept the same materials and elements in the design of the individual branches but they have chosen different colour combinations for each of them. The colour palette of the cladding of the corrugated sheet metal, the paintings, the ceramic tiles and also on the chairs is changing.

Architects have intentionally replaced the characteristic Mexican tiles by monochrome tiles and they have brought the touch of Mexico through some symbols typical for Mexico. The essential element is the cactus symbol, which is dominant in the interior and stylized in different forms. Other features include sombreros and garlands. The hanging lights are made of typical Mexican hats.

Reconstruction & Interior Design: **Studio Formafatal**
(Ing. arch. Dagmar Štěpánová & Ing. arch. Martina Homolková)
Photography: **BoysPlayNice (Jakub Skokan & Martin Tůma)**
Materials: **Ceramic Rectified Paving Ragno and Cement Screed (Floor); Ceramic Cladding Vogue, Corrugated Sheet Metal + Cut Self-adhesive Graphics, Dulux Painting (Walls); Steel Bars, Plywood + Black Oil, Solid Wood + Patina Work to the Desired Shade, Cor-ten Steel Sheet, Steel (Strip, Bent)**

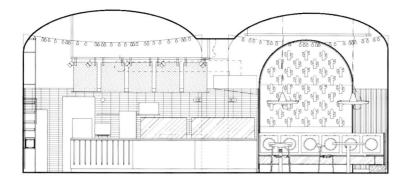

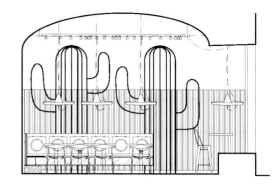

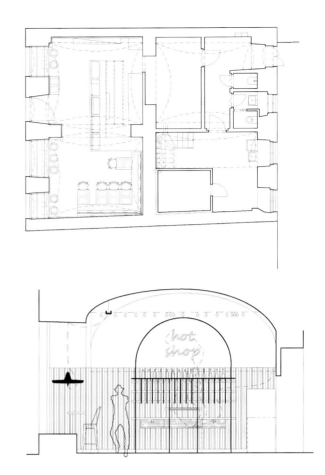

SUSHAN RESTAURANT

Area: **180 m²**
Location: **Chongqing, China**

Sushan restaurant is located in China's Chongqing Nanping square neighborhood, belongs to the high-end fast food take-away food brand, its mode of operation is online and offline. The restaurant's offline experience store is designed by Trenchant Design, and the concept of space is taken from the use of its VI and Daily Box indoors. The design of the flat design combines the space modelling, the idea of the creative and changeable outer band box shape throughout the interior design, to reinforce "Take Away" concept. The whole space is divided into the chef's area, the production area, the packaging area, the dining area and the outside of the dining room.

Design Agency: **Hangzhou Trenchant Decoration Design co., LTD**
Designers: **Qvent, Ling**
Materials: **Square Ceramic Tile, Steel Frame, Spell Water Grindstone, Exterior Wall Bomb Coating, Quartz Stone, Super White Glass**

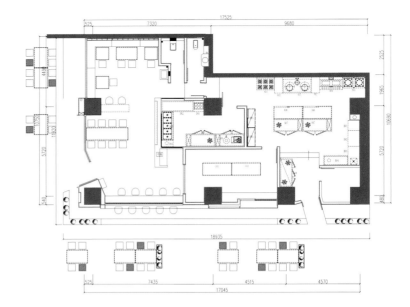

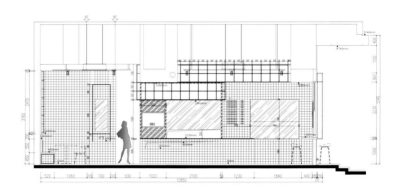

LIGHTS IN
THE ATTIC

Area: **132.5 m²**
Location: **Melbourne, Australia**

"Lights in the Attic" celebrates materiality
in raw and finished form. The original brief
called for an improvement of the current
spatial planning and to break away from
the monotony of Melbourne's "subway tile"
infatuation. Gently permeating imperfections,
reminiscent of the previous habitation were
unravelled to enrich aesthetic gestures,
connecting the planning and aesthetics both
visually and functionally. With the introduction
of fashion house finishes and motifs (such as
denim, and jewellery inspired pastry displays)
Architects EAT began to blur the lines
between retail and hospitality typologies and
a cross pollination of functionality and design
began to occur.

Design Agency: **Architects EAT**
Photography: **Derek Swalwell**
Materials: **Denim, Brushed Steel, Concrete**

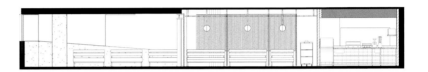

HAIDILAO HOT POT

Area: **340 m²**
Location: **Irvine, California, USA**

The design of the restaurant is a response to the location and program. The Chinese hot pot dining concept requires exhaust at each table. The upper floor location did not allow for the exhaust ducts to run underground, which meant vertical shafts had to be included in the design. The upper floor location in a busy mall required the design to be bold to draw people upstairs.

The grid layout of tables and shafts was embraced. The columns that shroud the shafts were made into a feature, which were connected with a trellis, highlighting the orthogonal layout. The colours and patterns of the wallpaper and wall tiles were inspired by Chinese pottery and graphics. The custom birdcage light fixtures are a direct reference to something one could find in a Chinese market.

Interior Design: **Beleco**
Architect: **Ignisio Studios**
Photography: **Bethany Nauert**
Client: **HaiDiLao Catering USA**
Materials: **Vinyl Tile, Shaw (Floor); Vinyl, Astek (Wallcovering); Design and Direct Source (Tile)**

TALK TO THE RED WALL—DOKO CHENGDU

Area: **200 m²**
Location: **Chengdu, China**

In the current popular catering culture, the importance of photographic space has become as important as the real existence of kitchen functions. In the process of space design, every link from concept to node needs to go through the deliberation of "photography is good-looking".

The name of this restaurant is actually a line of Tang Dynasty poem. The site is facing a Tang Dynasty buddha temple. Surrounded by the temple, the red wall leads the design of a signature view finder, which freezes outdoor scene for interior, also as lens, records customer's circulation for passers to better understand interior structure. This restaurant mainly provides Japanese fusion dessert. Metal net and glass curtain wall build up double facade for both the ground floor and the first floor.

Design Agency: **House Fiction**
Photography: **Tian Fangfang**
Materials: **Steel, Metal Net, Glass Curtain Wall Double Facade**

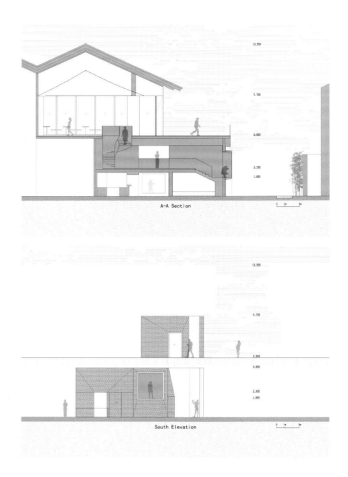

A-A Section

South Elevation

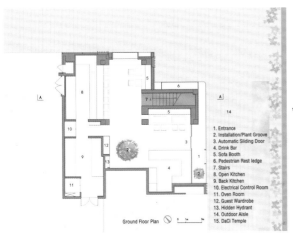

Ground Floor Plan

1. Entrance
2. Installation/Plant Groove
3. Automatic Sliding Door
4. Drink Bar
5. Sofa Booth
6. Pedestrian Rest ledge
7. Stairs
8. Open Kitchen
9. Back Kitchen
10. Electrical Control Room
11. Oven Room
12. Guest Wardrobe
13. Hidden Hydrant
14. Outdoor Aisle
15. DaCi Temple

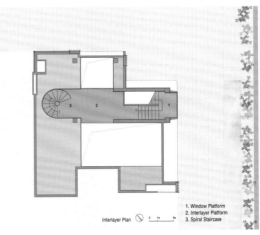

Interlayer Plan

1. Window Platform
2. Interlayer Platform
3. Spiral Staircase

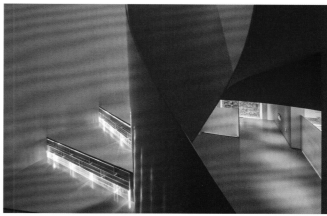

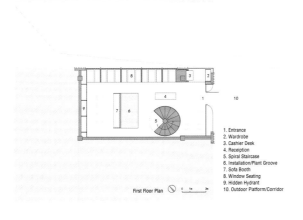

1. Entrance
2. Wardrobe
3. Cashier Desk
4. Reception
5. Spiral Staircase
6. Installation/Plant Groove
7. Sofa Booth
8. Window Seating
9. Hidden Hydrant
10. Outdoor Platform/Corridor

First Floor Plan

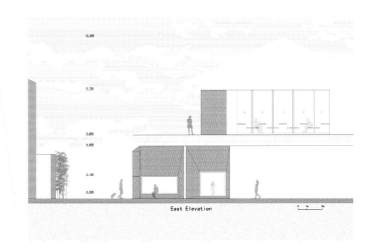

East Elevation

KHOSHA SPATIAL DESIGN

Area: **150 m²**
Location: **Beijing, China**

DTZW Studio regards space as a container of interesting stories. In this project, the designer Li Xibin combines Lanzhou's unique regional character with local food culture. He naturally integrates the regional culture and newly added designs into the original space, making entire renovation process like naturally growing out of it.

In repeated trials and comparisons, Li Xibin finds that the long table fits perfectly into the shape of the space, and the large-scale desktop adds great inclusiveness and possibilities. During meals, some interactions may happen between people around the table. The exchanges at large tables will vividly show local diets and Lanzhou's culture.

Design Agency: **DTZW Studio**
Leader Designer & Team: **Li Xibin**
Photography: **Xiazhi**
Partners: **Noah's Ark Decoration**
Clients: **KHOSA**
Materials: **Cement, Chaotic Aluminum, Gray Terrazzo, Led Decorative Screen**

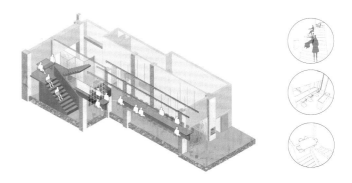

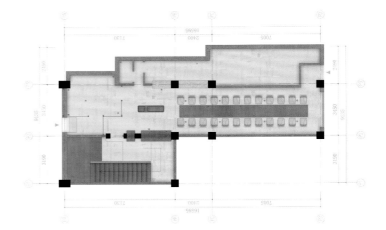

SO JEEZ
RESTAURANT

Area: **130 m²**
Location: **Chongqing, China**

The project is located in Chongqing city where have lots of historical buildings. The total area is 130 square meters with three arched doorways facing the street. The priority in the design of this project is "Subtraction", making complicated things simple, and to exploit the advantages of the historic streets. This project without many decorative elements, which can highlight the original charm of the space.

Design Agency: **Pure's Design Studio**
Interior Design: **Tianyu Xiong, Xiaokai Zhang**
Design Operator: **Hongda Lu**
Photography: **Xiaokai Zhang**
Materials: **Weathered Wood, Terrazzo, Stainless Steel**

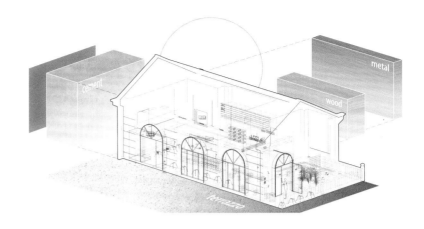

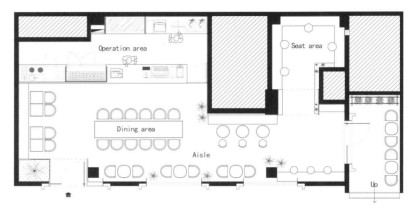

JOY BOX
RESTAURANT

Area: **160 m^2**
Location: **Taiyuan, China**

The project is located in Taiyuan, with an area of 160 square meters. The shape of the restaurant is a right triangle. The length of the side facing the street is as long as 20 meters, with 5.5 meters floor-to-ceiling windows. The key point of the designing of this project is to lower the sense of space aggression that is created by the shape of this project, and used the metal, catching the light, gaining the warmth.

Design Agency: **Pure's Design Studio**
Interior Design: **Tianyu Xiong, Xiaokai Zhang**
Design Operator: **Hongda Lu**
Photography: **Xiaokai Zhang**
Materials: **Terrazzo, Stainless Steel**

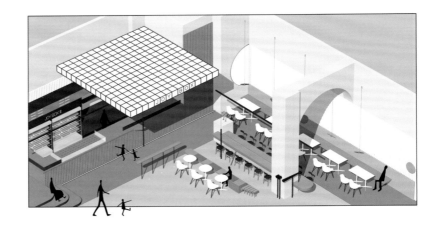

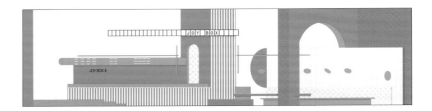

DINING BETWEEN LINES

Area: 152 m²
Location: **Shanghai, China**

After realizing a series of the Noodle Rack concept for Longxiaobao, a casual noodle diner, Lukstudio explores the lightness of the rack design at their first Shanghai location. Following the original fan-shaped plan, a curvilinear wooden core encases all service areas, allowing the white trapezoidal wireframe to stand out. Composed of 8mm × 8mm steel bars, the fine yet strong grid integrates partition, ceiling, seating and shelving, simultaneously blurring boundaries between diners and passers-by. Walking along the coherent storefront and seeing through the restaurant, in-line customers are encouraged to imagine themselves in place of the diners between the white lines. The soft barrier has shaped various spaces to suit different diners; may they be loners who enjoy their solitude, friends or strangers who connect over food. The dining experience is further enriched by hanging steel wires mimicking "the hanging noodles", a tribute to the previous concept stores.

Design Agency: **Lukstudio**
Director: **Christina Luk**
Project Team: **Jinhong Cai, Melody Shen, Leo Wang, Yiren Ding, Sarah Wang**
Photography: **Dirk Weiblen**
Client: **Longxiaobao**
Materials: **White Painted Steel Bars, Wood Flooring, Black Electroplated Stainless Steel, Black Tinted Glass, Gray Floor Tiles, Stainless Steel Wire**

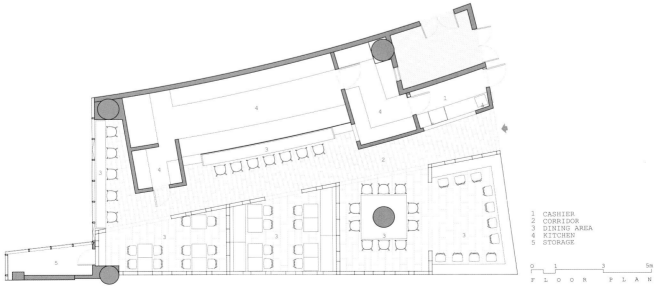

1 CASHIER
2 CORRIDOR
3 DINING AREA
4 KITCHEN
5 STORAGE

0   1   3   5m
F L O O R   P L A N

BIRCH
RESTAURANT

Area: **92 m²**
Location: **Saint Petersburg, Russia**

Birch is a restaurant of author's cuisine in the center of St. Petersburg, which was opened by 4 young chefs. It was decided that the restaurant would have two halls: The first is open to everyone, and the second is a secret hall with an open kitchen, where guests can come only for a set menu offered by the chef. The interior is built on a laconic combination of two basic materials: light wood, reminiscent of birch, and stainless steel, referring to the aesthetics of restaurant cuisines.

Interior Design: **Architecture bureau DA**
Photography: **Sergey Melnikov**
Materials: **Wood (Ashtree), Stainless Steel, Plaster Surfaces, Tiles, Panel of Wooden, Stainless Steel Cylinders**

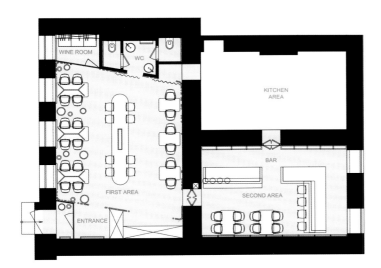

RESTAURANT 212

Area: **82 m²**
Location: **Amsterdam, The Netherlands**

212 is the address on the Amstel, but it also is the balance between two passionate chefs joining forces to create one unforgettable experience. The focus of the interior is on the central kitchen and guest experience; everything else is literally greyed out. The interior layout is designed around the open kitchen in the centre of the space. The counter wraps around the kitchen on three sides in an interrupted U-shape. On the corners, the counter top cantilevers over the edge of the counter to create tables of two or four. The back wall boasts all major appliances and an open fireplace.

The choice of materials has been kept pure and honest: stainless steel for the entire kitchen, rear wall and hood. Natural oak is used for the counter top & front as well as the floor and ceiling as a warm counterpart to the industrial feel of the kitchen. The centre ceiling and bar counters have a custom three-dimensional surface constructed from oak pyramid shapes to create a warm, dimmed and intimate ambiance.

Design Agency: **concrete**
Design Team: **Rob Wagemans, Tobias Koch, Sylvie Meuffels, Erik van Dillen**
Photography: **Wouter van der Sar**
Materials: **Stainless Steel, Oak Parquet, Grey Voiles, Grey Carpet, Three-Dimensional Oak Pyramids**

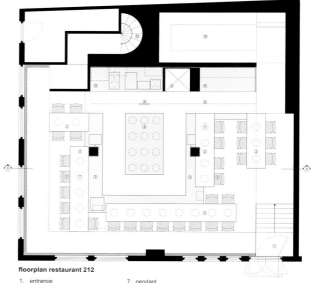

floorplan restaurant 212

1. entrance
2. bar table
3. kitchen bar
4. kitchen center block
5. bar stool
6. neon logo
7. pendant
8. hood
9. open fire place
10. back of house kitchen
11. kitchen
12. staircase to toilet and winecellar

section restaurant 212

1. to staircase
2. bar table
3. kitchen bar
4. kitchen center block
5. bar stool
6. neon logo
7. pendant
8. hood
9. open fire place
10. to back of house kitchen

0 m   5 m

MAMA MAKAN DUTCH-INDONESIAN GRAND CAFÉ

Area: **385 m²**
Location: **Amsterdam, the Netherlands**

Mama Makan is a contemporary Dutch-Indonesian Grand Café that seamlessly integrates with the hotel lobby, connecting travellers with the local residents and the historic context of the neighbourhood. Mama Makan is inspired by the journeys on the ancient trading routes. The restaurant is located in the traditional 'Plantage' quarter associated with its heritage in Dutch trading and collection, specifically by boat, in the Far East.

A brass cage-like cabinet wrapped around the core hides the structure of the building. The cage circles around the core, with a concrete-edged palm pattern as a backdrop, organising the restaurant, bar and lobby areas. This cage accommodates all basic functions such as the restaurant bar, chef's tables, private dining, wine fridges, wardrobe, service stations and the open show kitchen. In addition typical Asian cooking equipment and herbs collected during the Dutch travels can be found. Moving outwards towards the glass facade, the restaurant features various seating areas.

Design Agency: **concrete**
Design Team: **Rob Wagemans, Tobias Koch, Sofie Ruytenberg, Zana Josipovic, Johanna Zychski, Marlou Spierts, Cathelijne Vreugdenhill**
Photography: **Wouter van der Sar**
Client: **aedes real estate / hyatt**
Materials: **Floor Tiles Ceramic, Wooden Floor, Brass Cage Shelving, Graphic Concrete**

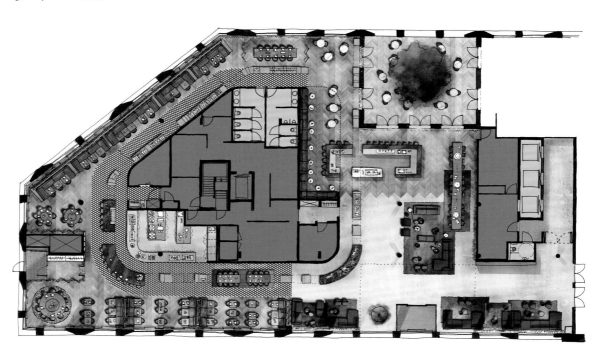

SUPERBABA

Area: **167 m²**
Location: **Victoria BC, Canada**

The interiors of Superbaba reference the strong arch motifs in traditional Middle Eastern architecture as well as quirky details found in diners and eateries. This nod to the traditional is offset with bold, contemporary colours of varying shades of blues, greens and pinks painted on the walls and used in the counter, shelving, and seating millwork. Plants, hand painted signage and warm lighting create a relaxing and comfortable atmosphere. The large Superbaba neon sign along with the light boxes on the exterior reference the neon seen everywhere in fast-casual spots in the Middle East.

Creating a comfortable and intriguing space that was at once functional proved an interesting challenge. Working within a relatively small budget, designers had to be very creative with materials and how they articulated the details. This meant working with typical utilitarian details and actualizing them in a more deliberate and artful way.

Interior Design: **Studio Roslyn**
Project Team: **Kate Snyder, Jessica MacDonald**
Brand & Graphic Design: **Superbaba In-house Design Team**
Photography: **Lauren D Zbarsky**
Materials: **Confill to Texture the Walls, Oak Wood, Laminate, Black Powder Coated Steel Tube Paint**

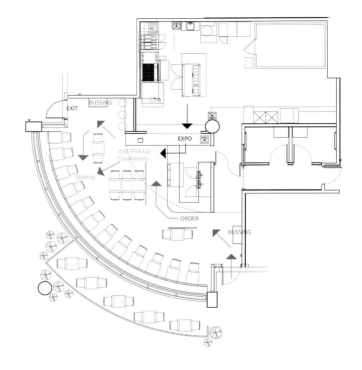

TATSU RAMEN

Area: **390 m²**
Location: **New York, USA**

With an overall minimalist aesthetic, light wood tones, and monochrome colour palette infused with pops of red; the restaurant builds upon the existing Tatsu Ramen brand. The interior architecture draws inspiration from Japanese origami, with folding planes that peel back to reveal other textures. Accent lighting adds to the dramatic quality of the folds and punctuates the space. An intricate Samurai dragon mural by artist Kozyndan etched in black metal serves as the focal point of the dining area while the openness of the kitchen brings patrons into the action.

Design Agency: **Studio UNLTD**
Architecture: **New York Design Architects**
Kitchen Designer: **Singer Equipment**
Photography: **Scott Morris**
Artwork: **KozynDan**
Materials: **Plaster, Ash Wood, Wood Flooring, Laser Etched Metal Laminate Panels, Wall Tile**

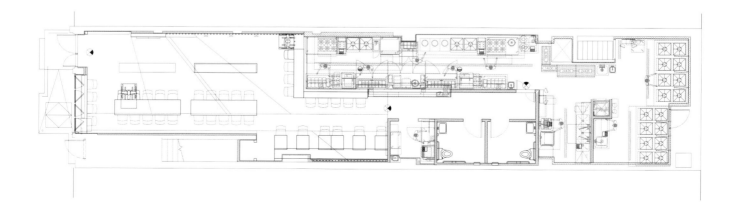

ZVD

Area: **250 m²**
Location: **Kyiv, Ukraine**

This is a meeting place for the like-minded people, connoisseurs of American style, modern pop and hip-hop culture. The establishment is cozy, bright, rich in elements and various photo zones. Meeting the needs of guests, it is modern and flexible for hosting events of different formats. Textures and finishes are from natural materials: wood, metal, leather. The colour scheme is of sand shades. Such palette unveils an open space during the day, and conveys reflections of neon lights at night. The restaurant is divided into three rooms, each with its own theme and seating arrangement. While first and second room are light and open, the third is executed in dark colours and well suited for evenings, with more private and intimate atmosphere. The most striking elements of decor are tumble dryers with rotating drums, and Mars and Pepsi vending machines doors, which conceal WC block behind them. This 24/7 downtown establishment represents a strong visual image referring to American culture.

Design Agency: **balbek bureau**
Architects: **Slava Balbek, Nastya Mirzoyan, Yulia Barsuk**
Photography: **Yevhenii Avramenko**
Materials: **Wood, Stainless Steel, Eco Leather, Concrete**

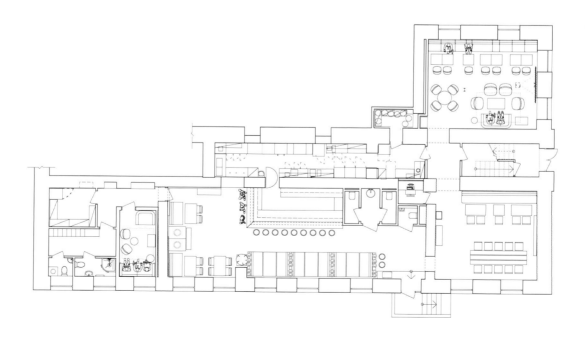

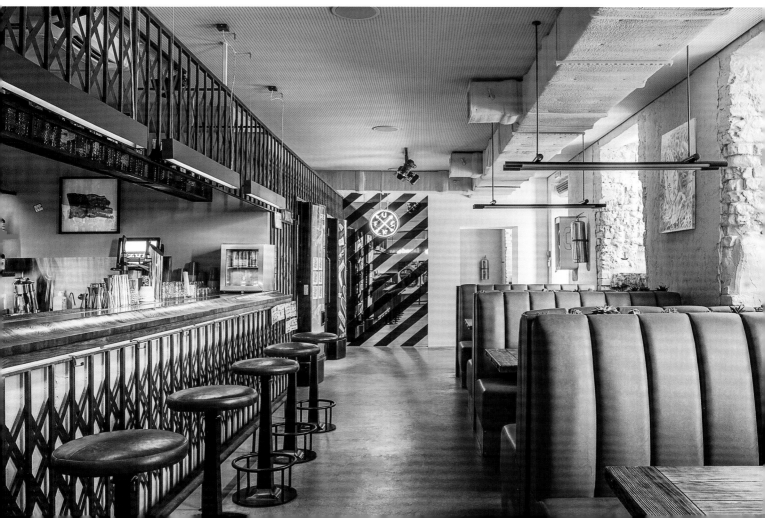

REDOUBLE FISH

Area: **450 m²**
Location: **Shantou, China**

The Redouble Fish (For exquisite design, DDDBrand changed "Red double fish" to "Redouble Fish") design is the product of a new national fashion combining Chinese traditional art with contemporary cultural exchanges. Designers hope to show the synesthesia effect of eating through the brand. Meanwhile, consumers can experience tangible products and intangible culture to enjoy the concretization and abstraction.

Design Agency & Interior Design: **DDDBrand**
Interior Photography: **POPO Image**
Materials: **Loam Wall, Solid Wood**

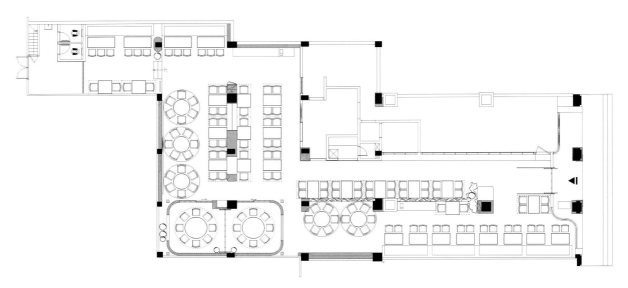

GWANGHWAMUN HAE-MUL

Area: **182 m^2**
Location: **Seoul, Republic of Korea**

Facade in front of the building was constructed in a two-story building to overcome its narrow drawbacks compared to the size of the building, and a fish formation was hung on the second floor to indirectly express the feeling of a seafood restaurant.

The space was divided into large halls, kitchens, and rooms, and counters were installed in the center of the customer's line considering two entrances. And the room can be used as a separate room for six people, and the wall between the room and the room can be used as a group up to 18 people, and the hall and the room boundary did not look like a room. The hall was also constructed of fixed-type partition seats on one wall of the hall, and the space next to the counter was designed to make a single-seat table long to widen the choice for various customers. Traditional wooden structures in the form of gable have been refined to the extent of strengthening the structure, and used as elements that allow vertical viewing of the hall space and showing the past.

Design Agency: **GONGSANGPLANET**
Design Team: **Kim Kyoung Mok, Heo Sung Young**
Photography: **Choi Yong Joon**
Materials: **Wood Floring, Cement (Floor); Brick, Wood, Oldwood (Wall); Exposure Structure, Paint (Ceiling)**

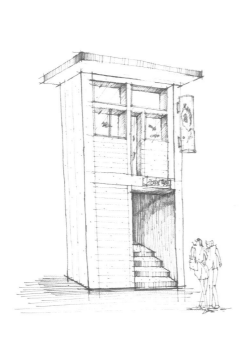

1. ENTRANCE
2. SUB ENTRANCE
3. AQUARIUM
4. HALL
5. BAR
6. KITCHEN
7. SUB KITCHEN
8. ROOM1
9. ROOM2
10. ROOM3
11. M-TOILET
12. W-TOILET

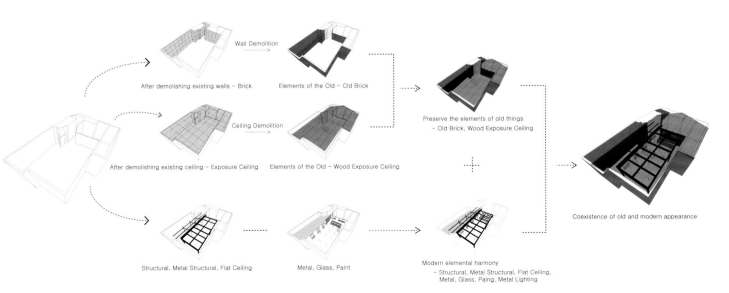

After demolishing existing walls – Brick

Wall Demolition

Elements of the Old – Old Brick

After demolishing existing ceiling – Exposure Ceiling

Ceiling Demolition

Elements of the Old – Wood Exposure Ceiling

Preserve the elements of old things
– Old Brick, Wood Exposure Ceiling

Structural, Metal Structural, Flat Ceiling

Metal, Glass, Paint

Modern elemental harmony
– Structural, Metal Structural, Flat Ceiling,
Metal, Glass, Paing, Metal Lighting

Coexistence of old and modern appearance

TANG HOTPOT

Area: **330 m²**
Location: **New York, USA**

Tang Hotpot is conceived as a place of Reversed Fusion, where contemporary design is assimilated into an ancient dining tradition to create an exciting experience of both history and modernity. At the entrance bar, a tunnel made of copper tubes frame the circulation into the main dining area while supporting custom-made ceramic artifacts. The main dining area with a spectacular 20 feet high ceiling, is characterized by its semi-circular banquette seats surrounding the hotpots. The design team highlights the space not only with the shimmering copper pots crafted by traditional artisans, but also with the floating copper mesh screen in front of the background wall with an interplay of walnut, painted brick and copper framed mirrors. The central wall of the dining space features a contemporary play of Tang Dynasty mural. The private dining mezzanine with a fantastic view overlooks the main dining area and the busy Chinatown streets.

Design Agency: **New Practice Studio**
Photography: **Montse Zamorano**
Client: **Tang Hotpot**
Materials: **Walnut wood, Copper, Aluminum mesh, Weathering steel, Clay plaster**

ROBATAYAKI GENROKU / KAISEKI SHAKUHACHI

Area: 173.3 m²
Location: **Chengdu, China**

There are two categories in this project with a single kitchen, one is for the Japanese-style barbecue Robatayaki, and the other is for Kaiseki which is a traditional Japanese meal brought in courses. In the part for Robatayaki, Tsutsumi & Associates installed an aged wooden frame in the utmost height, then put the mirror on the ceiling to show dynamic reflected image. On the wall facing the street, windows and washi light box are set in checkered pattern, and those directional light raise the wooden frame elegantly. In the part for Kaiseki, Tsutsumi & Associates overlapped tilted ceilings that is a typical language of traditional tea-room. These ceilings has different angle each other, and those caused moire pattern into the space.

Interior Design: **Tsutsumi & Associates (Yoshimasa Tsutsumi, Weiwei Shi, Yu Peng)**
Photography: **Liu Wei**
Materials: **Hinoki Wood, Yakiita Wood, Copper, Granite, Diatomite, Mortar**

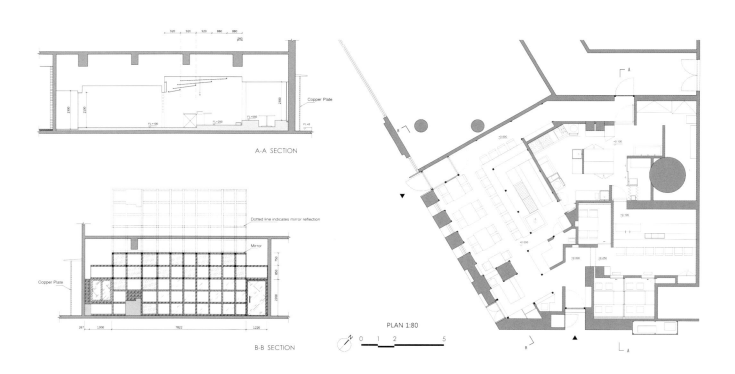

A-A SECTION

Copper Plate

Dotted line indicates mirror reflection

Mirror

Copper Plate

B-B SECTION

PLAN 1:80

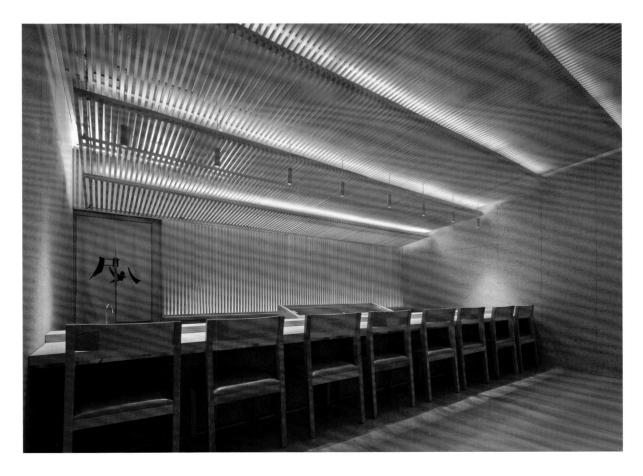

MANZO LIANG MA QIAO

Area: **360 m²**
Location: **Beijing, China**

This project is a Japanese restaurant that serves many kinds of sake. For expressing sake, Tsutsumi & Associates defines main concept as "water stream" which is a very important essence of sake. On the wall of hall, Tsutsumi & Associates created waterfall by putting wooden louver which is consist of straight bars and a various length of tapered bars and LED glazer light being shot down from top of the louver wall. The wall of the VIP room is same as that of the hall, besides a various length of order-made frosted acryl edge lighting emphasizes the concept of "water stream".

Interior Design: **Tsutsumi & Associates**
Photography: **Misae Hiromatsu, Yuming Song (Beijing Ruijing Photo)**
Materials: **DI-NOC Film, WPRC, Black Coloured Glass, Granite, Tile, Mortar**

01 waiting space
02 cashier
03 drink bar
04 sushi bar
05 kitchen
06 sofa area
07 VIP room
08 private room
09 tatami room
10 hall
11 toilet
12 back space
13 fish tank

PLAN
0 1 2 4

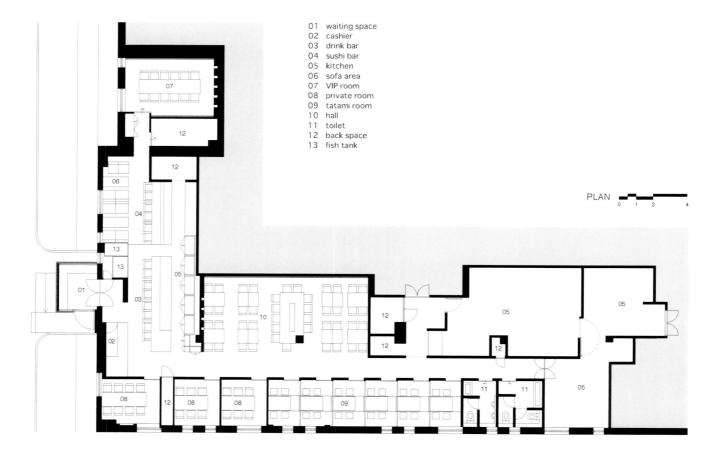

IZAKAYA RESTAURANT

Area: **325 m²**
Location: **Munich, Germany**

The Japanese stand-alone restaurant IZAKAYA, located in the building of Hotel Roomers, announces its presence to the guests at the moment of arrival, with the show kitchen visible through the glass facade of the porte-cochere from Hotel Roomers Munich. The restaurant itself is composed of an array of black materials, with a contrasting feature of light wooden lamellas along the ceiling and wall towards the kitchen. The space is structured into two zones by a solid seating booth element in the centre. A three-step level change separates the bar zone at the entrance from the quieter restaurant zone in the rear.

The rotating vertical panels in the centreline of the booth element can connect or separate the space depending on the angle of rotation. One side of the panel features a Japanese-inspired artwork on silkscreen by artist Gijs Scholten. In the early evening, the whole space can appear as one. After restaurant hours, the bar can be closed off to establish a darker and cosy mood that lasts deep into the night. The eye-catcher of the restaurant zone is the oversized wooden koi-carp lamp by LZF above the long table.

Design Agency: **concrete**
Design Team: **Rob Wagemans, Tobias Koch, Nuria Ripoll, Kasia Heijerman, Marlou Spierts, Johanna Zychski, Maike Daemen, Mark Haenen, Hilka Ackermann, Ulrike Lehner, Sofie Ruytenberg, Zana Josipovic**
Artist: **Gijs Scholten (Silkprinted on Rotating Panels)**
Photography: **Steve Herud**
Client: **ggch / gekko group**
Materials: **Bespoke Furniture, Bartop in Backlit Marblo, Wooden Lamella Ceiling, Gold Mirror Walls, Bespoke Floor Tiles, Backlit Ricepaper Wall**

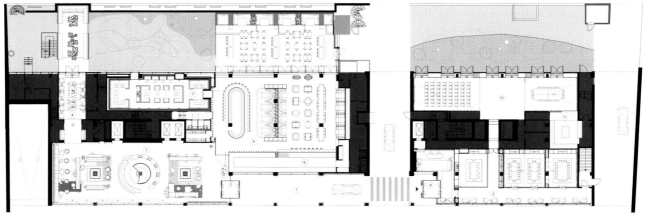

ground floor plan

landsberger straße

0 m — 5 m

1. drive way with vegas ceiling
2. hotel entrance
3. lobby
4. library
5. izakaya restaurant and bar
6. open kitchen
7. hidden whiskey room
8. event spaces entrance
9. meeting rooms
10. ballroom
11. show kitchen

MOMOFUKU LAS VEGAS

Area: **700 m²**
Location: **Las Vegas, Nevada, USA**

Momofuku is by nature understated with its interiors, instead putting the emphasis on its food and service. As a result, the design brief was to maintain the brand's clean aesthetic, which is defined by a white oak material palette and clean simple details.

To present Momofuku in Las Vegas, DesignAgency began with the brand's signature palette of architectural white oak, and to make it location-specific, they added a few playful materials, such as a peach-tinted mirror, brass accents and warm neon lighting. They layered in some not-so-serious elements such as custom-designed carpets with dragons chasing peaches, and original artworks including a 50-foot long mural by American multi-media artist David Choe and Korean artist Kwangho Lee's crimson knitted chandelier that resembles a dragon guarding the Secret Private Dining Room.

Design: **DesignAgency**
Photography: **Nikolas Koenig**
Client: **Momofuku**
Materials: **Coverings Etc. (Main Washroom Materials), Fireclay Tile (SPDR Washroom Walls), Design & Direct Source (SPDR Washroom Floors), Banquette Leathers (Bennett Mills Agency), Secret PDR Banquette Upholstery (Maharam)**

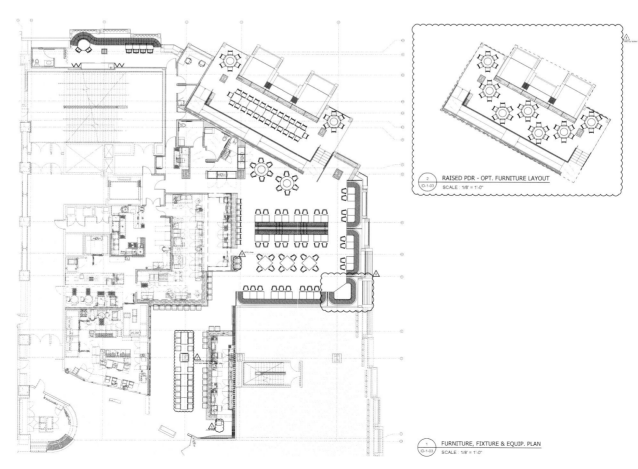

2   RAISED PDR - OPT. FURNITURE LAYOUT
ID-1-03   SCALE 1/8" = 1'-0"

1   FURNITURE, FIXTURE & EQUIP. PLAN
ID-1-03   SCALE 1/8" = 1'-0"

GWANGHWAMUN MONG-RO

Area: **297 m²**
Location: **Seoul, Republic of Korea**

When the designers first visited the scene, the most impressive scene was not the modern buildings that were built recently, but rather the spaces that could be described as some old-looking buildings from the passage of time and a small shelter between them. The designers wanted to melt the comfortable feeling into the space, so they decided that the concept was "the change in space due to the passage of time, the similarity to the surroundings."

To express these images, they built a small building in the center of the space, representing one small building wall and ceiling of the building, representing the skin of the skin peeled, and the other walls and ceilings made a hole in the surface of the roof to create a light that leaked out. Then, thick trees that feel the years inside and outside of small buildings were naturally installed to express the space between them. The expression of this expression was not an expression of unfamiliarness by expressing foreign food, but rather a bit trimming and melting hands, giving the impression of familiarity and comfort to Koreans.

Design Agency: **GONGSANGPLANET**
Design Team: **Kim Kyoung Mok, Im Su A, Yang Jung Mo**
Photography: **Lee Pyo Joon**
Materials: **Epoxy, Tile (Floor); Cement, Brick, Fire screen, Tree, Moss (Wall); Moss, Fire Screen (Ceiling)**

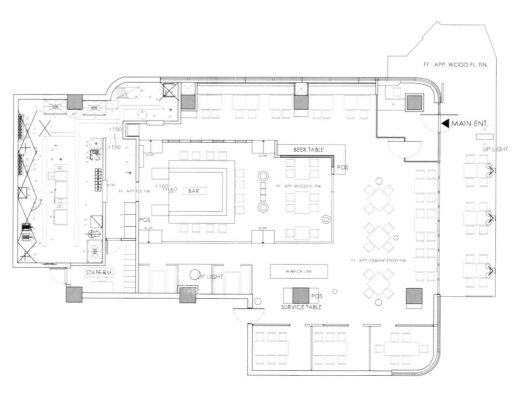

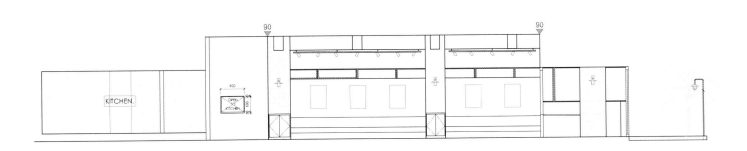

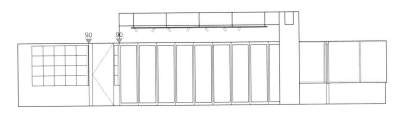

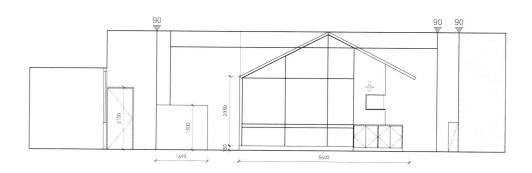

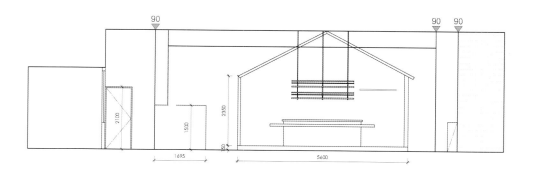

HUMANS
SEAFOOD BAR

Area: **285 m²**
Location: **Moscow, Russia**

Yuna Megre (Megre Interiors) designed Humans
Seafood Bar as an artistic representation of
the underwater world, reminding of the origin of
the humankind. The dark-grey textured walls of
concrete with color runs peak through the mesh
structure symbolizing the foaming waves of
the ocean. The rivers of glass flow through the
cracked openings of elm tree table tops connecting
them into a single visual stream. This brutality is
embanked by soft velvet banquettes that frame
the restaurant perimeter. The lighting is dark and
subdued and flickers reflections through the wire
mesh creating an almost ocean like movement.

Design Agency: **Megre Interiors**
Designer: **Yuna Megre**
Photography: **Mikhail Loskutov**
Stylist: **Dasha Soboleva**
Materials: **Wood (Elm Tree), Marble, Brass, Concrete,
Velvet, Canvas (Fabric Texture), Wire Mesh (On the Walls
and Ceiling), Artificial Plants and Greenery**

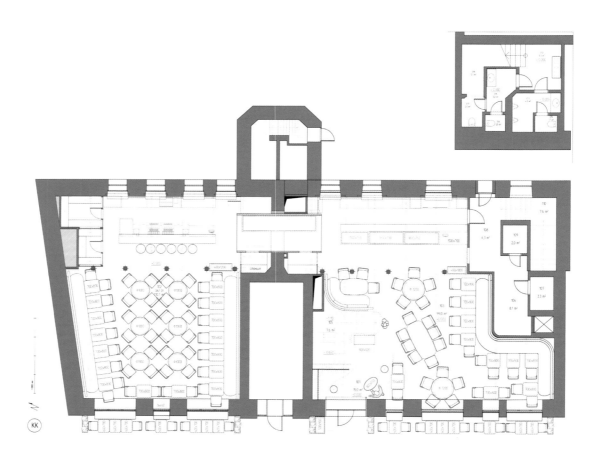

KIDO SUSHI BAR

Area: **80 m²**
Location: **Saint Petersburg, Russia**

A small sushi bar, which is part of the KIDO network, is located in one of the dormitory districts of St. Petersburg. In this project it was very important to make an interior that would instantly attract the attention of passing by and driving by public to a new place.

As a basis there was a rather small and simple space. Architecture bureau DA wanted to save this simplicity and make the main emphasis on a really unusual, memorable structure. Thus, an impressive wooden construction was created, located opposite the panoramic windows, consisting of more than 400 volumetric triangles.

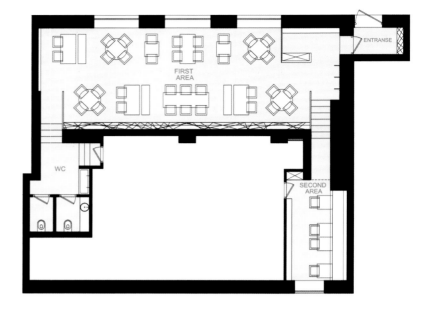

Interior Design: **Architecture bureau DA**
Photography: **Boris Lvovsky**
Materials: **Brass Perforated Partition, Black Marble, Velvet, Brass, Mirror Ceiling**

RAMEN MUSASHI

Area: **115 m²**
Location: **Hangzhou, China**

Menya Musashi is one of famous Ramen brand from Tokyo, Japan. As the top-level of Japanese ramen, designer utilized simple lines to represent the eaves of the Japanese building, and then divide and recombined the space, tried to bring the scene of japanese old town street which full of lanterns at sunset into dining space.

Go into the dining space, a great quantity of gratings and colour assortment (wood and white) has brought a strong impact of Japanese style. There is a ring bar in the middle of space which is a micro landscape with innumerable mountains and valleys by using moss and stone. Among this area, the design team not only decorates space lively, but also makes people and food, people and space to interflow on their feeling and mood.

Design Agency: **Golucci International Design**
Chief Designer: **LEE Hsuheng**
Design Team: **Zhao Shuang, CHAO Chong**
Photography: **Luluxi**
Client: **Ramen Musashi**
Materials: **Aluminum Square Tube with Wood Pattern, Blue Tile, Sandstone Paint, Carbonized Wood**

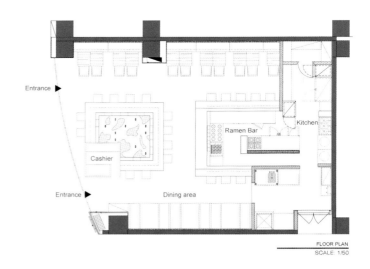

FLOOR PLAN
SCALE: 1/50

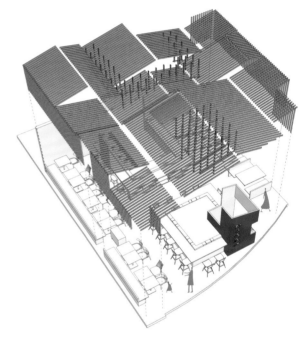

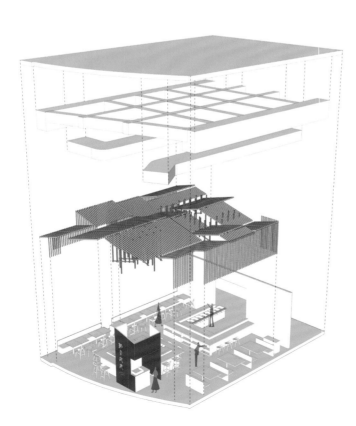

KAIKAYA

Area: **125 m²**
Location: **Valencia, Spain**

Kaikaya, is the result of this history, bringing the fusion of traditional and methodic Japan with the tropical and exotic, contemporary Brazil to the center of Valencia. A representation showed both through its kitchen as well as through its design as described afterwards.

The design needed to contain a strong splash of colour, together with an eclectic style that could mix the 2 concepts of Japan + Brazil without being conventional. Masquespacio designed the restaurant by the use of materials that remind to Japan like wood and raffia, together with elements that bring in the tropicalismo from the samba country with its colourful patterns made of mosaic tiles, parrots and an overwhelming incorporation of plants.

Design: **Masquespacio**
Photography: **Luis Beltran**
Client: **Kaikaya**
Materials: **Metals, Raffia, Paint, Tiles, Coloured Concrete, Oak, Plants**

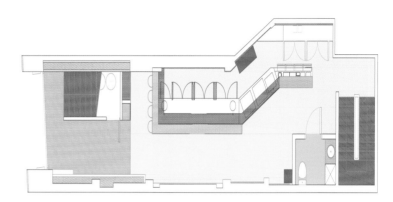

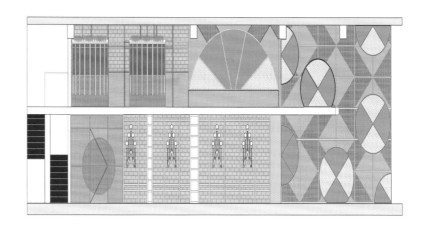

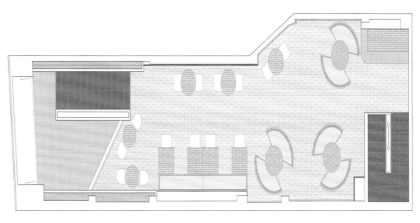

THE GOOSE HUT BISTRO (APM BEIJING)

Area: **280 m²**
Location: **Beijing, China**

The Goose Hut Bistro is a restaurant of creating heart habitat. Utilizing the space to express culture and change people's lifestyles is real design. That is the responsibility the designer should take. The plan of this project is a rectangular site, which is not easy to bring designers inspirations and it is difficult to seek the design breakthrough to some extent. Houses and trees are the two major visual symbol of the restaurant.

The kitchen bar is kept as the service room; the three round sofas in the back of the restaurant represent the principal house. The left two groups of long sofas represent Western-wing house. The main kitchen and two compartments are regarded as Eastern-wing house. Fortunately, the spatial design of Goose Hut Bistro encountered Beijing traditional courtyard, then a few trees in the middle of the yard have become the essence of whole restaurant. The concept from bird house is transformed into the installation art of the Bird's Nest in the dining space.

Design Agency: **Golucci International Design**
Design Team: **LEE Hsuheng, ZHAO Shuang, ZHENG Yanan, MA Dongjie**
Photography: **Luluxi**
Client: **The Goose Hut Bistro**
Materials: **Aluminum Square Tube with Wood Pattern, Aluminum Board, Oak Wood Flooring, Copper, Sandstone Paint**

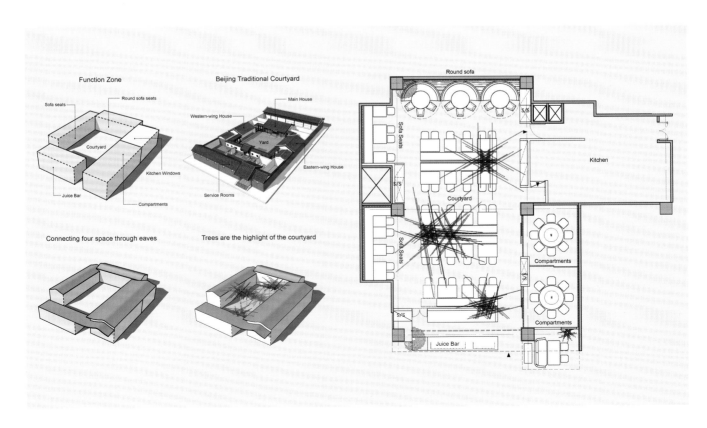

RUA DA CUNHA MACAU HOTPOT

Area: **680 m²**
Location: **Beijing, China**

Rua da Cunha Macau is a hotpot restaurant next to CCTV. At the initial stage of design, the design team determined to use glass curtain landscape area as the breakthrough point. By using the original subsidence space to create a Miniature Theater, from the lowest point (French windows) to highest point (interior space), which forms three levels, at the same time, each one could appreciate fine scenery. The rest space of this restaurant is more private, which are suitably used as compartments. Meanwhile, it can improve the efficiency of the whole space. They mainly used the logs, other natural materials and the most primitive methods to create a rich spatial effect.

It is worth mentioning that the facade. The original red line is half curve, which is bound to be planarization and cannot be combined with interior space. Since designers changed the curve into a broken line, which makes plain facade variable and full of the sense of rhythm.

Design Agency: **Golucci International Design**
Design Team: **LEE Hsuheng, Zhao Shuang, Chou Tsungi, Zhou Qiuxia, Zhang Chao**
Visual Designer: **Chou Tsungi**
Photography: **Luluxi**
Client: **Rua da Cunha Macau Hotpot**
Materials: **Aluminum Square Tube with Wood Pattern, Terrazzo, Copper Plate, Walnut**

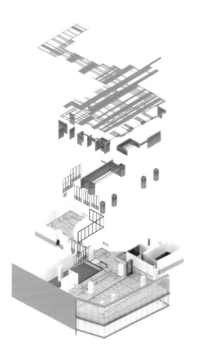

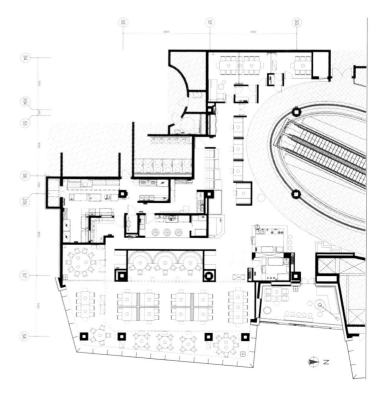

HUAYUE COURT

Area: **850 m²**
Location: **Shanghai, China**

Huayue Court focuses on integration and inheritance of traditional Chinese cuisine which includes Beijing Fruitwood Roast Duck, Huaiyang and Northern cuisine. What's more, it also joins Guangdong and Sichuan special local foods. That brings different food mix and unique dining experience. This is no doubt the fusion of food and the collision of taste buds.

Designers divided the whole space (over 600 square metres) by using semi transparent screens and Chinese garden windows. Creating a picture in the scene and a scene in the picture, both of them complement each other, forming a wonderful visual centre. Through the new expression of traditional garden, Huayue Court brings diverse Chinese style. In order to make the traditional Chinese elements embodied in contemporary form, designers created the ink and dye pattern on embossed glass and combined the British lattice with sofa cloth. Between tradition and modernity, in the East and the West, Huayue Court finds a perfect balance.

Design Agency: **Golucci International Design**
Design Director: **LEE Hsuheng**
Design Team: **LEE Hsuheng, Zhao Shuang, Zhang Chao**
Photography: **Luluxi**
Client: **Huayue Court Peking Duck Restaurant**
Materials: **Metal-cut Chinese Window, Stone-cut Chinese Window, Grey Marble, Inkjet Wall**

CHUAN'S KITCHEN

Area: **450 m²**
Location: **Foshan, China**

As bamboo is the most common material
and symbolic extraction of Sichuan
culture, the restaurant takes Sichuan
Qingshen's Bamboo-weaving Art as the
medium and carries out the intangible
culture of Sichuan with tangible material.
Bamboo-weaving stretching through
the space and cuisine with hearty flavor
satisfy both appetite and spirit. The
dim light matches concrete furnishing,
reflecting the coexistence of elegance and
vulgarity of Sichuan cuisine. Joined by
the communicators, users and viewers of
culture with thousands of years of history,
the contemporary aesthetics of traditional
delicacy is now taking shape.

Design Agency: **Infinity Mind**
Bamboo-Weaving Artists: **Zhai Guihua, Wei Baijn,
Liu Qianxing, Song Libin, Xu Donglan, Liu Pan,
Liu Junxi**
Photography: **Cao Haochang, Ba Songyang**
Client: **Guangzhou ABO Food & Beverage
Management Co., Ltd.**
Materials: **Bamboo, Concrete**

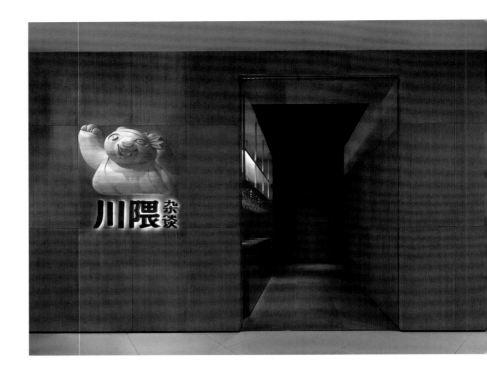

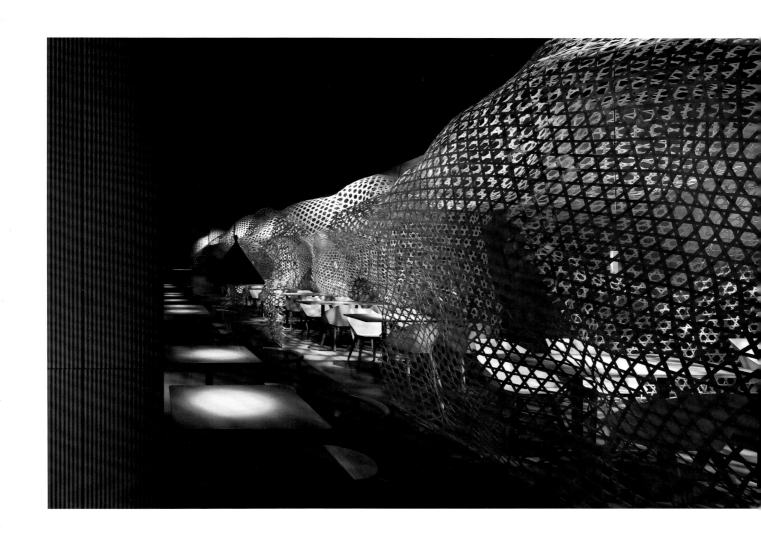

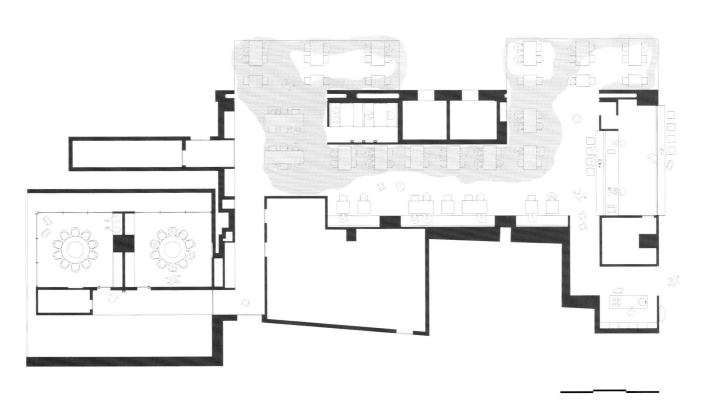

SPICY NOSPICY

Area: **200 m²**
Location: **Kyiv, Ukraine**

Asia in "Spicy NoSpicy" is feeling not only in taste, but also in the interior. The wood of a neutral warm colour is balanced by cold aluminum panels with a matte finish, and bright decorative blotches (grids on the ceiling, green plants, carving on columns), like spices in dishes add completeness to the whole image.

The forming element of the interior has become a large-scale installation on the ceiling from 600 decorative bamboo fishing nets, specially brought from Vietnam. Restaurant is also decorated with 8 carved wooden columns, which holds the ceiling. The presence of panoramic windows in conjunction with artificial light directed through the grids on the ceiling create the impression of staying in a Vietnamese bungalow, through the rushy roof of which is punched sunlight. In the evening the atmosphere of the restaurant is fundamentally changing: the light, sifted through the grids, forms on the tables and columns mysterious shadows, thereby creating an appropriate atmosphere of chamber and comfort.

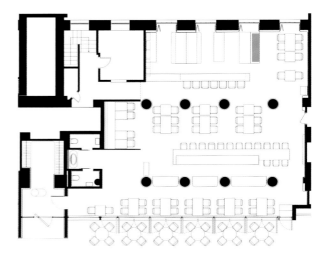

Design Agency: **YOD Design Lab**
Photography: **Andriy Bezuglov**
Materials: **Veneer Sheets, Wooden Array, Satin Aluminum, Brick, Self-leveling Floor, Bamboo Nets on the Ceiling**

L28 CULINARY PLATFORM

Area: **280 m²**
Location: **Tel Aviv, Israel**

Named after its location on the city's lively Lilienblum Street, L28's design starting point was a glass "fishbowl" on the sidewalk amongst historical buildings. The goal was to give the space both warmth and neutrality in the design. An elevated platform with lounge seating and dining tables encloses the main floor of the restaurant giving the main floor a certain privacy from the street. Timber slats of wood span the ceiling and create hanging arches and partition walls that communicate the various different seating areas within the double-height space. The density and positioning creates undulating patterns while also controlling the light and views. The restaurant's main seating area is gathers around the open kitchen and bar and a private dining area is located on a mezzanine level. Natural and warm materials are used, such as the slatted wood panels, leather upholstery, smooth resin floor and black steel. A green wall is incorporated at the back of the restaurant, while shelves planted with herbs and spice plants are placed in front of the bar and kitchen.

Architecture: **Kimmel Eshkolot Architects**
Design Team: **Etan Kimmel, Limor Amrani, More Gelfand, Yoav Ronat, Corvin Matei**
Project Management: **Yaron-Levy**
Lighting Design—Restaurant: **Orly Avron Alkabes**
Photography: **Amit Geron**
Client: **Start Up Nation Central**
Materials: **Wood, Resin Floor, Concrete, Black Steel, Greenery**

Gallery Floor

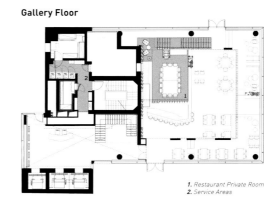

1. Restaurant Private Room
2. Service Areas

Ground Floor

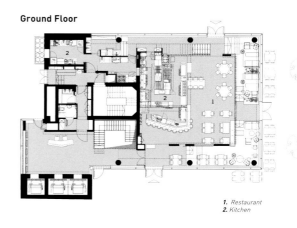

1. Restaurant
2. Kitchen

RUSKI
RESTAURANT

Area: **1037 m²**
Location: **Moscow, Russia**

Ruski restaurant boasts of unrivaled panoramic views of Moscow city and holds the title of the highest restaurant in Europe. It seems to be floating on air—the space is bright and breathtaking.

The elegant modern atmosphere of the restaurant is a post-avantgard interpretation of Russian culture and corresponds perfectly to its spirit, offering guests traditional Russian cuisine with a modern twist. The restaurant not only has the only fully open display kitchen where the whole process of food preparation can be spectated by guests but has a wood burning traditional Russian pechka, to which a whole section of the menu is dedicated. With the kitchen at its core, the guest zones are positioned to take the benefit of the 360 degree views of the city from a position so high, that sometimes it's above cloud.

The restaurant is split into 4 zones of the natural elements, paying homage to the Russian pagan culture. The kitchen is fire, the ice bar is water, with 2 enclosed dining halls taking earth and air. They are all brought together by the light color scheme. Brass, chrome, stone and spectacular beauty of distressed wood, form the unique style of the restaurant where most elements are bespoke and were created by Yuna Megre for this project.

Design Agency: **Megre Interiors**
Designer: **Yuna Megre**
Photography: **Sergey Ananiev**
Stylist: **Natasha Onufreichuk**
Materials: **Agate Stone, Distressed Wood, Brass, Mesh, Textile Ropes, Crystal and handblown glass (Chandeliers), Ice (Bar), Concrete, Green Malachite Stone, Stucco**

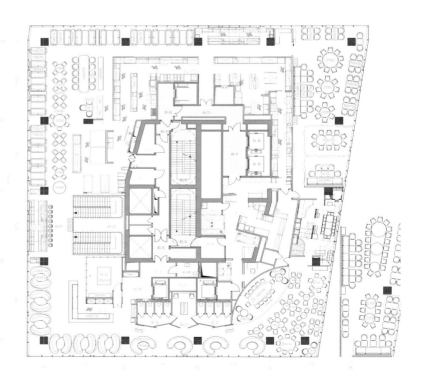

GRANDMA'S HOME RESTAURANT

Area: **400 m²**
Location: **Hangzhou, China**

How to break through the stereotype impression of Chinese restaurants and bring it closer to the taste of the emerging young consumer groups? They look at the complex words, images and purposes behind "Grandma's Home" restaurant and explore to sort out and express a line of clues, for example, the emotions implied by the symbol "grandmother's home", impression of Chinese restaurants, and its slogan which indicates unique landscape features of Jiangnan, the region south of the Yangtze River. In the fast-paced restaurant industry in China, it is their wish that diners could experience fashionable and unique attentiveness and care in this reputable and affordable restaurant chain.

Design Agency: **Hangzhou AN Interior Design CO.,Ltd**
Architect: **Weng Shanwei**
Photography: **Yujie Liu**
Materials: **Mirror of Stainless Steel, Aqua Green Terrazzo, Hand-plaited Bamboo**

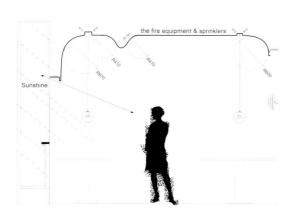

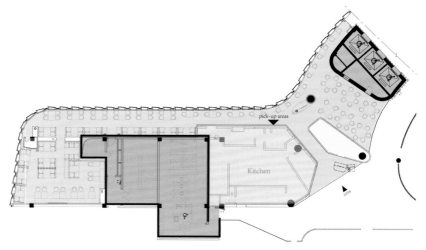

SONG CHINESE CUISINE

Area: **2280 m²**
Location: **Guangzhou, China**

Song's Chinese Cuisine uses modern materials and design techniques to interpret Chinese restaurants. 100,000 pieces of heterosexual stainless steel bricks and 400,000 pieces of coloured feathers constitute the basic form of the Song's Restaurant. The curving shape of the surface breaks the imagination of the Chinese restaurant and creates a unique spatial experience.

As the guests walk through the restaurant, the space gradually becomes narrow; it can be in close contact with the feathers, and the feathers that have been cast at high temperature slide over the fingertips. The smooth feathers leave the residual temperature in the hands. The stainless steel brick wall, seamless, hard, smooth; the brick floor of the collage has traces of years of friction, and the interspersed body makes the interior energetic.

Design Agency & Interior Design: **Republican Metropolis Architecture**
Photography: **Jack Qin**
Client: **Song Chinese Cuisine**
Materials: **Glass, Stainless Steel**

WALL

DEFORMATION

EXOGENIC ACTION

FINAL RESULTS

WALL

DEFORMATION

EXOGENIC ACTION

FINAL RESULTS

CANYON

HUMAN AND SPATIAL RELATIONSHIP

HUMAN AND SPATIAL RELATIONSHIP

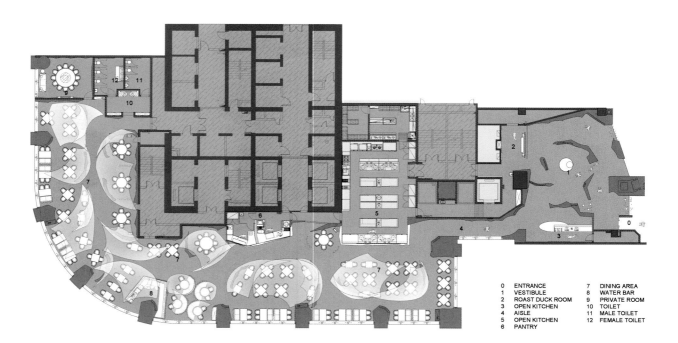

0	ENTRANCE	7	DINING AREA
1	VESTIBULE	8	WATER BAR
2	ROAST DUCK ROOM	9	PRIVATE ROOM
3	OPEN KITCHEN	10	TOILET
4	AISLE	11	MALE TOILET
5	OPEN KITCHEN	12	FEMALE TOILET
6	PANTRY		

RYBA-PYLA

Area: **240 m²**
Location: **Kyiv, Ukraine**

The name of fishbar "Ryba-Pyla" in Ukrainian translation means "Sawfish". But at the same time in the Ukrainian language the phrase "Ryba-Pyla" also has another meaning like "fish drank", and arises an association that the fish is drunk, that is "drunk fish".

The brutally ironic interior fully supports the concept of a fish bar. Among the main conceptual elements are stylized skeleton of sea creature under the ceiling in the middle of the main hall, as well as installations on the walls and lamps from rusty circular saws, that metaphorically associated with the name of establishment. In decoration applied rusty metal and old wood, supposedly from the influence of seawater. Old container blocks, bought in stock and re-assembled already on this place, became the adornment of one of guest halls.

Design Agency: **YOD Design Lab**
Photography: **Andriy Bezuglov**
Materials: **Decorative Plaster, Sheet Metal Oxidized like Corten, Board of Solid Wood, Container Blocks, Stainless Steel Sheet, Prof Flooring, Bulk Concrete Floor**

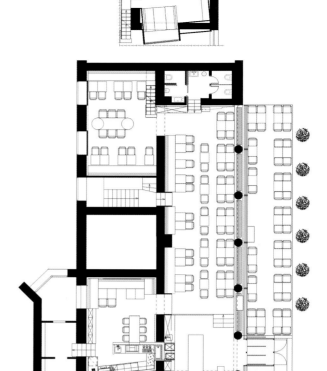

MUST

Area: **400 m²**
Location: **Kyiv, Ukraine**

MUST is a premium steak house in the center of Kyiv, Ukraine. Wood, leather, glass, stone, metal are typical materials for the classic steak house, but in MUST they are presented atypical that distinguishes it and makes more modern. By analogy with carbonized grilled steak, YOD used a burnt blackwood in the interior. Like burnt on steaks from grill grates the charred boards cover walls and its texture creates a delicate and restrained basis for lighting.

Light in restaurant is soft and accentuated, so every table turns out to be zoned in twilight. Hanging lamps, filed by garlands over groups of tables, made according to the sketches in the form of pelvic bones. The accent of main hall is a huge chandelier with diameter of 3 meters from glass bones and skulls of different animals, made specifically for this object by a Czech partner. On the second floor there is a bar with myxology, unique light show and music. Its atmosphere is complemented by the installation of 28 thousand coins, which is in constant motion thus creating dynamics suitable for bar.

Design studio: **YOD Design Lab**
Architectural Concept: **Bureau Zotov & Co**
Photography: **Roman Kupriyan, Andriy Bezuglov**
Materials: **Wood Board, Glass Blocks, Tempered Dyed Glass, Marble, Veneered Panels, Decorative Concrete Blocks, Marble, Board of Solid Wood, Bulk Concrete Floor, Acoustic Panels on the Ceiling**

1. Main hall of the bar
2. Technical premises
3-4. WC
5. Dressing room in WC
6. Washer

Total area (without terraces): 116,50 м²
Number of landing places: 38

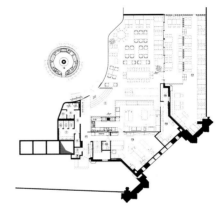

1. Main hall of the restaurant for 74 seats
2. Cash desk
3. Hallway
4. Utility room
5. Men's WC
6. Dressing room in men's WC
7. Dressing room in women's WC
8-10. Women's WC
11. Hallway
12. WC
13. Kitchen
14. Washer
15. Wine cellar
16. Champagne bar for 16 seats
17. Terrace

Total area (without terraces): 398,20 м²
Number of landing places: 90

PIZZA 22

Area: **350 m²**
Location: **Moscow, Russia**

Complex geometry and longstanding history of the premises have become the key starting points in space planning decision during development of the design for pizzeria Pizza 22. Pizza 22 is located in the historical center of Moscow, in the premises of a former salt storage. At the same time, with only one third of the premises located on the ground floor, the main part thereof is located below the ground level in the former salterns.

The most challenging task was to create colourful and attractive planting in the semi-basement of the premises at the level of 6.5 meters. To make the guests feel in these rooms as comfortable as on the ground floor, the design team housed an open kitchen in the lowest room, arranged lots of tubs with trees, which create the being-at-the-ground-level effect, and also used an installation of a bright art object in the form of red staircase, which became the central element of the room. The ultimate interior is light, minimalistic and not overloaded with details.

Design Agency: **Architecture bureau DA**
Design Team: **Anna Lvovskaia, Boris Lvovskiy, Fedor Goreglyad, Maria Romanova, Aliaksandra Bialkova**
Photography: **Sergey Melnikov**
Materials: **Metal, Wood, Concrete, Decorative Plaster, Cracked Tiles**

ELEVATION -5.685

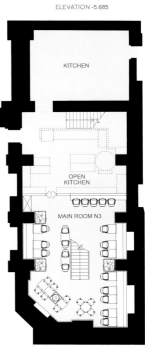

KITCHEN

OPEN
KITCHEN

MAIN ROOM N3

ELEVATION 0.000

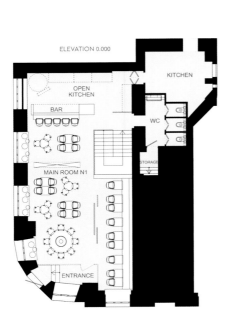

OPEN
KITCHEN

KITCHEN

BAR

WC

STORAGE

MAIN ROOM N1

ENTRANCE

ELEVATION -2.840

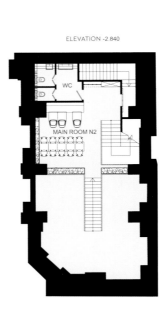

WC

MAIN ROOM N2

MERKATO

Area: **740 m²**
Location: **Valencia, Spain**

Taking advantage of the industrial space of an old aircraft hangar, with their former lives in the subconscious, the design of this new gastronomic market and restaurant, situated in central Valencia is based on historical and culinary sensibilities of the city. With the helping hand of Valentín Sánchez Arrieta the studio has created a renewed market concept based on honesty, both in materials and products. Logically, efforts have been made to maintain the industrial nature of space without falling into topics, thematization or traditions.

Design Agency: **Francesc Rifé Studio**
Designer Team: **Carlos Fernández Saracíbar, Sergio Alfonso, Bruno Benedito, Patricia Guridi, Jessica Machucala, Paola Noguera, Sonia Pellicer, Stefanos Sideroglou, Nùria Pedrós**
Collaborating Architect: **Murad García Estudio**
Photography: **David Zarzoso**
Materials: **Terracotta Tiles, Poplar Wood, Metallic Trusses, Pine Wood**

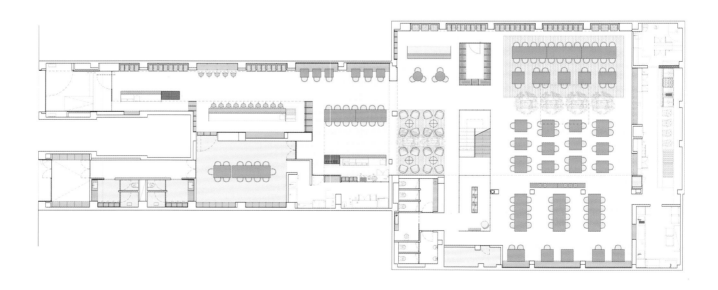

VARIATION IN THE CRACK • PARK QIAN

Area: **420 m²**
Location: **Xingyi, China**

Park Qian is a group. They set up their own catering brands in 2018, using their unique perspectives and experiences to make interesting attempts in their hometowns, gradually forming their brand culture through new spaces and cuisines.

The folding blocks linked to the exterior intend to expand the visual length. When you enter the building, you will see the same white blocks immediately, which stick into the folding area. The stack light and original thick sense form the box to the second floor. These sections form the weightless experience, and the sunlight between the cracks also strengthen the sculptural sense. When you reach the center of this building, as the drinking area, the central bar counter is also inserted into the folding blocks. Meanwhile, the bar counter balances the customers on both sides, which forcibly cut off the space, thus, there are jet lag for the two sides.

Design Agency: **FON STUDIO**
Design Team: **Jin Boan, Li Hongzhen, Luo Shuanghua**
Photography: **FON STUDIO**
Client: **Park Qian**
Materials: **Floor Slab, Steel Board, Synthetic Quartz**

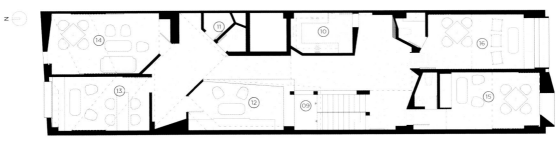

2nd Floor Plan

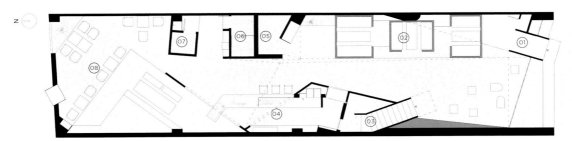

1st Floor Plan

① Entrance	② Booth area	③ Staircase	④ Bar	⑤ Exhibition	⑥ Male toilet	⑦ Female toilet	⑧ Scattered area
⑨ Staircase	⑩ Kitchen	⑪ Toilet	⑫ Box A	⑬ Box B	⑭ Box C	⑮ Box D	⑯ Box E

0   1   2   5m

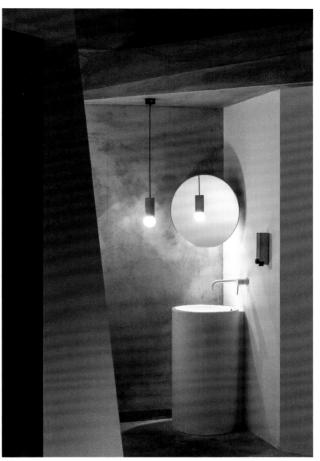

XIAMEN HAIGAN XIAOYOUYU SEAFOOD RESTAURANT

Area: **1200 m²**
Location: **Xiamen, China**

The project was repurposed from a former factory terrace. The unique location and unconventional structure of the original space allowed the designer to give full play to imagination and creativity. At the entrance, the flexible cut spatial block, dilutes the massiveness of the building, which is just like a modern installation art work full of tension, leading the space to extend inward with its clear lines.

Within the space 4.6 meters high, a two-story structure was built in the atrium. The designer ingeniously created an open door way in this area, which seems to bring people into another dimension. Under the staircase, there is a separate sunken area, deep and tranquil, waiting for foodies to step in. With minimal and refined designs colliding with the space, and modern life style integrating with the local culture of respecting and enjoying the nature, a modern yet elegant dining destination eventually came into being.

Design Agency: **Xiamen Fancy Design & Decoration Co., Ltd.**
Interior Design: **Fang Guoxi, Xie Chenyang**
Photography: **Jin Weiqi**
Materials: **FOREX Cement Boards, FORMICA Wood Veneers, BAOWU Steel Panels**

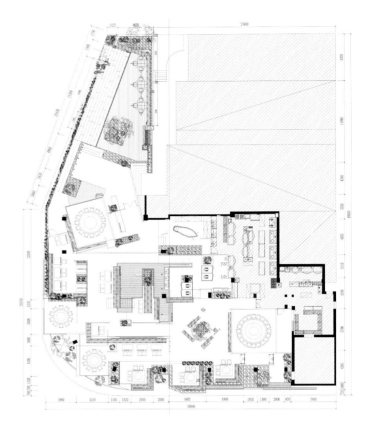

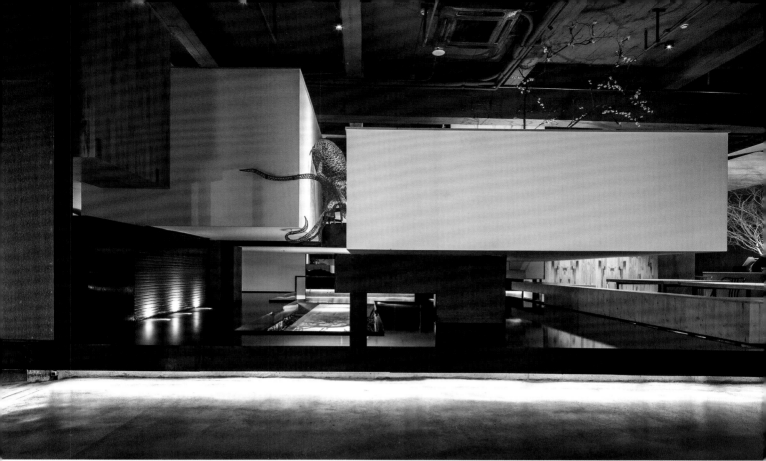

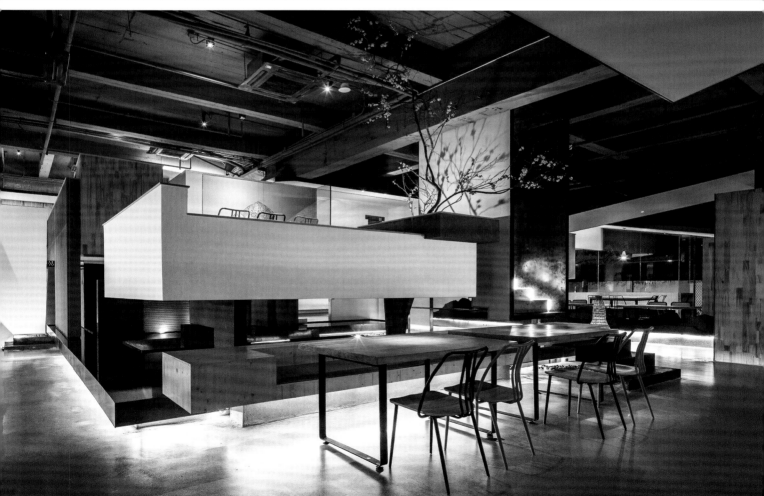

GOOSE HUT HUNAN CUISINE

Area: **500 m²**
Location: **Beijing, China**

Goose Hut season store is located in Beijing city center—Beijingfun, which has a special geographical location and Beijing style cultural resources. Time and time again, the team discussed the concept of designing and tried to create courtyards in the whole restaurant. The yard is the goal concept, and then designers rebuilt the new spaces (rooms and compartments) in this garden. All the corridors formed by Chinese gallery bridges, which is a wonderful idea. When people enter the space from several entrances, they won't feel it like a restaurant, but only a part of the garden, could be a house, landscape, an art or a yard. People will never see the whole view when they walk into this space. Some of them can't find the entrance and exit or even lost their way. It's lovely to be lost in such a wonderful garden.

Design Agency: **Golucci International Design**
Design Director: **LEE Hsuheng**
Chief Designer: **ZHAO Shuang**
Design Team: **MA Dongjie, WU Shangyong, ZHENG Yanan**
Photography Art Pics: **Santiago Barrio (Spain)**
Photography: **Lulu Xi**
Materials: **Chinese Old Gray Brick, Aluminum Board, Oak with Wood Pattern, Walnut, Sandstone Paint**

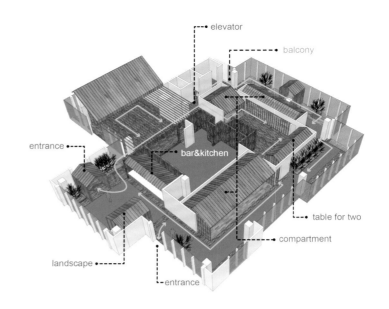

Restaurant kitchen is covered with gray bricks, and other spaces are connected by one continuous wall.

In order to create the warmth of home. We place several small houses and landscapes in restaurant.

The structure of each house has its logic.

space perspective

LA SPEZIA

Area: **350 m²**
Location: **Sumy, Ukraine**

La Spezia is an Italian restaurant, located in Sumy, Ukraine. Creating this facility, YOD did not set a goal to surprise by design, first and foremost they focused on the potential audience and its needs. They achieved their goal and the result speaks for itself: Today La Spezia is a successful restaurant and a favorite place for many inhabitants of the city.

The restaurant is divided into two halls: day and evening. The day hall is main, it is spacious and bright, with lots of green plants and with panoramic windows, through which inside the room enters a lot of sunlight. The unifying element of hall became a structural wooden grid on the ceiling, which hides engineering and with greenery "refreshes" the whole space. The second hall in trattoria is decorated in dark colours, it has a more chamber atmosphere, therefore it is especially popular in the evening. Its accent is the communal table located in the center and it can be used as a single company and people unfamiliar with each other.

Design Agency: **YOD Design Lab**
Photography: **Roman Kupriyan**
Materials: **Self-leveling Floor, Wooden Array, Wooden Veneer, Natural Greens, Marble**

1. Entry
2. Dining hall 1
3. Dining hall 2
4. Dining hall 3
5. Private dining hall
6. WC
7. WC
8. Kitchen

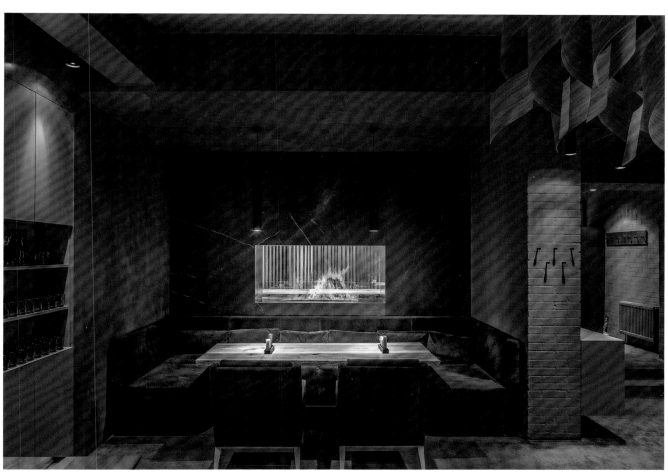

BAVEL

Area: **669 m²**
Location: **Los Angeles, USA**

The design of Bavel embraces the regions from which the cuisine is derived, interpreting those ideas through the lens of its Arts District location. The worn brick warehouse which houses the space, served as a wonderfully textured canvas for the restaurant to evolve from. Natural light served as the critical ingredient employed to make the dining room bright and inviting atmosphere with natural light from skylights, storefront openings & clerestories. The interior brick walls are treated with a wash which evokes the textures of ancient Middle Eastern seaside villages. The centerpiece of the design are planters which hang just below the massive skylight.

Design Agency: **Studio UNLTD**
Architecture: **Osvaldo Maiozzi**
Landscape Designer: **Steve Siegrist**
Kitchen Designer: **Alec Bauer of KRBS**
Photography: **Tanveer Badal**
Materials: **Decorative Tile at Walls and Floors, Concrete at Floors, Plants, Brick Walls, Steel Storefront, Marble Bar Top, Acoustic Plaster, Decorative Living Glass**

COBRA LILY

Area: **442 m²**
Location: **Shanghai, China**

Cobra Lily is a Pan-Asian restaurant and bar located in Shanghai's popular Xintandi complex. Designed around a mysterious femme fatale, the design is a journey through her day and the places she hangs out.

The original early 1900's decorative Chinese archways have been kept creating a secret alleyway. Opening into this grand alleyway you discover the bar and lounge area. A two-storey atrium complete with a floating DJ booth creates a dramatic entrance. Lounge and dining areas sprouting from this area to form intimate pockets of dining space. Upstairs diners nestled in the top of the atrium look down over the lounge and bar area. The bathrooms are positioned at the end of a long dark corridor with secret agent themes. Raw concrete mixed with sleek finishes create an upmarket urban chic in a relaxed setting.

Interior Design: **hcreates**
Photography: **Seth Powers**
Materials: **Brick, Custom Tile, Custom Wallpaper, Brass, Various Fabrics, Steel**

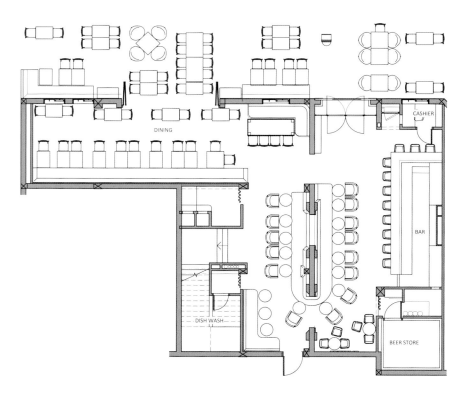

ON TAP
FOUNDERS SUMATRA BROWN ALE
CONTENDER EXTRA PALE ALE
BCB PILSNER   HELLES LAGER
WHITE IPA   BREWDOG STOUT
RINGSIDE RED   SUCKER PUNCH PA
DECEPTION ALE   MORNINGTON PA

COBRA LILY

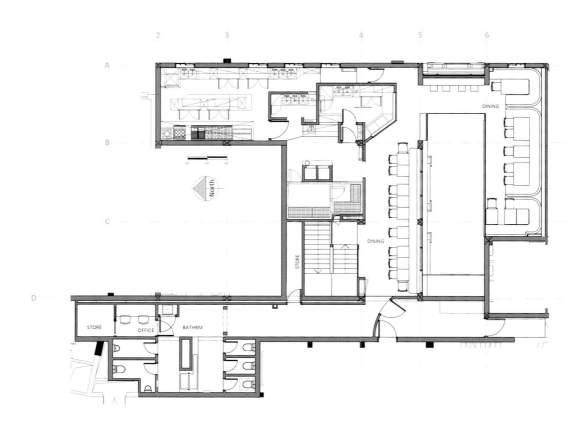

RESTAURANT KOMPANIYA

Area: **300 m²**
Location: **Saint Petersburg, Russia**

Kompaniya Restaurant on Moskovski prospect is the fourth project that Architecture bureau DA has developed for the restaurateurs Aleksei Krylov and Aleksandr Prokofev who are well-known in Saint Petersburg. Key element of the interior is space itself. On the one hand the designers wanted to make the most of double height space. On the other hand, show connection between the two levels of the restaurant.

Interior Design: **Architecture bureau DA**
Photography: **Sergey Melnikov**
Materials: **Metal, Concrete, Solid Oak, Coloured Concrete Tiles**

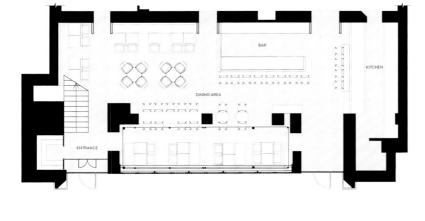

NĂM • MODERN VIETNAMESE CUISINE

Area: **575 m²**
Location: **Kyiv, Ukraine**

NĂM • Modern Vietnamese Cuisine is a restaurant of modern Vietnamese cuisine in Kyiv. Interior of NĂM restaurant is decorated in French colonial style with characteristic ethnic blotches. In order to achieve maximum authenticity YOD tried to apply as much as possible natural materials in decoration, which were specially aged according to conditions of tropical Vietnamese climate. All wooden products including parquet on the ground floor were made from massive 100-year old barrels from under white and red wine. Almost every element in design with the exception of chairs and technical lighting was created exclusively for this restaurant.

On the first floor interior space forms by open kitchen, thanks to which guests can observe processes of cooking their meals. Due to experiments with light restaurant radically changing its image according to time of day. Thanks to large windows, all halls of restaurant are full of light In daytime. With onset of twilight, lighting becomes more muted, and closer to night it is almost completely extinguished, leaving only certain accents and shadows that provides a complete transformation of restaurant's atmosphere in evening.

Design Agency: **YOD Design Lab**
Graphic Design: **PRAVDA design**
Photography: **Andriy Bezuglov**
Materials: **Wooden Products from Old Wine Barrels, Plaster, Cement Based Tiles, Brass, Marble, Self-leveling Floor, Leather, Wicker Items Made of Artificial Rattan**

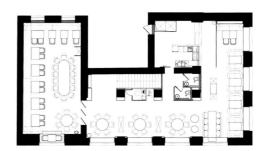

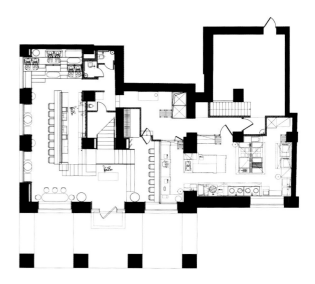

PESCE AL FORNO

Area: **435 m²**
Location: **Odessa, Ukraine**

Pesce al Forno (Fish on Fire) is the Italian fish restaurant of known restaurateur Savelii Libkin. The name of the institution primarily reflects its general concept. Into this concept is laid both a way of cooking on fire in the furnace and that the materials used in the decoration had undergone heat treatment too: the floor is covered with a heat-treated ash tree, walls—by burnt with different gradient copper squama, and also the countertops are made of stones and heat-treated massif.

In creating the interior of the restaurant YOD tried to portray the marine theme through a series of associations. The whole restaurant is like "woven" from fishnet: the concept of the first floor forms a scale knitted installation from ropes that cover the entire ceiling. The ceiling resembles the surface of the seabed with craters of underwater geysers, from which hang the round glass lamps—the images of poured from glass floats for nets used previously by sailors. In the kitchen fully opened to visitors, as if just caught by the same fishnet on ice are presented the fresh fish and other sea delicacies.

Design Agency: **YOD Design Lab**
Photography: **Roman Kupriyan**
Materials: **Wood, Ropes, Copper, Cast Forms of Glass (Glass Lamps), Plaster**

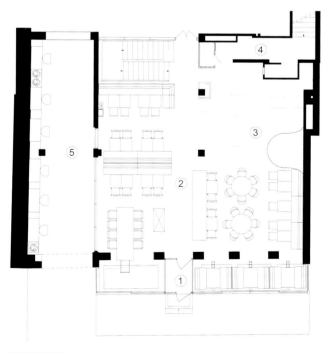

FIRST FLOOR

1. Entry hall
2. Main hall
3. Open kitchen
4. Kitchen
5. Summer terrace

- Total guest's first floor area - 135 m²
- Total first floor area - 192 m²
- Total first floor seat capacity - 64

CELLAR FLOOR

6. WC
7. Kitchen
8. Main hall
9. Bar

- Total guest's cellar floor area - 150 m²
- Total cellar floor area - 240 m²
- Total cellar floor seat capacity - 66

HOLY CHICK

Area: **300 m²**
Location: **Kyiv, Ukraine**

Holy Chick is a restaurant that tactfully combines frank rudeness with the elegance of classical elements. The very name of the restaurant already indicates the guest that its format and kitchen are devoted to chicken—its main product.

From the entrance reveals the ironic character of the concept of the establishment: the ground near the entrance is the embodiment of such a "glamorous" chicken house, and the door handle on the front door is executed in the form of the famous gesture of Winston Churchill's "victory hand". In the interior are hidden various "Easter Eggs" imperceptible at a glance. It's no coincidence are woven classical chandeliers from wire, because this material is the main on the poultry factory. The bathrooms are laid out by the white square tile, doors are made from stainless steel, which generally resembles the industrial rooms in the poultry farm. In addition the hall on the ground floor is decorated by wall panel in the form of classical eggs cells from concrete.

Design Agency: **YOD Design Lab**
Photography: **Roman Kupriyan, Andriy Bezuglov**
Materials: **Carpet and Stone Coating, Plaster, Recycled Board, Wooden Array, Brushed Aluminum, Stainless Steel, Wire, Leather**

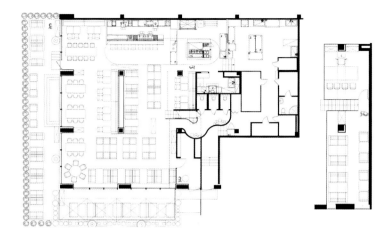

PARK HOUSE FOOD MERCHANTS

Area: **600 m²**
Location: **Sydney, Australia**

Park House Food Merchants is a 200-seat restaurant on Sydney's northern beaches. Conceived as a loft style art warehouse, it is a sympathetic interpretation of the old motel through 70s costal and retro styling. An expressive and artistic insertion into the building's existing shell this restaurant is part art gallery, part loft and all motel charm. This project represents 1 of 6 stages of work carried out as part of a gateway project to the greater Mona Vale precinct. The venue has proven to perform as a community hub, its social role highly visible.

Architecture & Interior Design: **Alexander &CO.**
Editorial Styling: **Claire Delmar**
Art Curation: **Dani Butchart, Makehaus**
Photography: **Felix Forest**
Materials: **Custom Design Carpet by Passo Flooring, Oregon Timber by Nash Timber, Recycled Mixed Species Hardwood Original by Ironwood Australia**

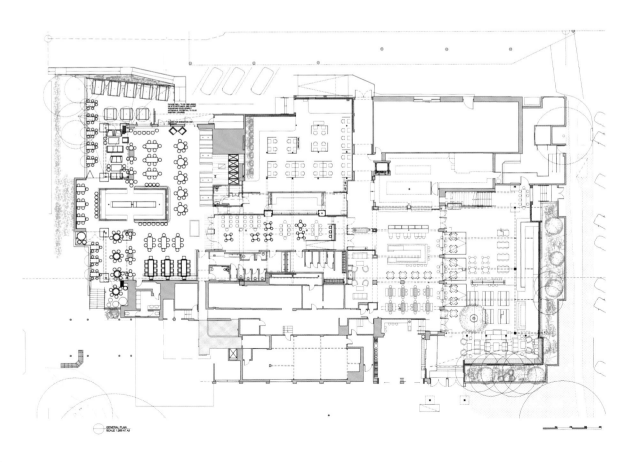

GENERAL PLAN
SCALE 1:200 AT A3

DONG PHU 1932– VIETNAM CUISINE RESTAURANT

Area: **440 m²**
Location: **Ha Noi, Vietnam**

Many people wonder why the restaurant was named Dong Phu 1932 among thousands of another beautiful names. Dong Phu is the own name of the house is located at 12 Hang Dieu, Ha Noi city. And Le House selected this place to build the Dong Phu Restaurant. A house with beautiful French architecture was built in 1932. Through many ups and downs of history, the house is a symbol of Ha Noi ancient streets.

The impressive façade is a large wooden door, engraving details from the old furnitures. Every interior decoration is created by crafting skills, such as: Embroidery Art and Glass Painting Art. These paintings look like from to folk to the royal. The main material is old brick without plastering and sorted by random as children's puzzle. The moss wall is carefully taken care of. That makes visitors realize the ancient of the house. And finally, the important thing Le House is trying to create a feeling—A feeling of the TRUE!

Design Agency: **Le House**
Photography: **Tuan Dao Studio**
Materials: **M&A Art Tiles—Handmade Ceramic and Brick Concrete, Hai Long Glass—Tempered Glass, Custom Metal Art, Rusted Steel Material with Hanging Tree**

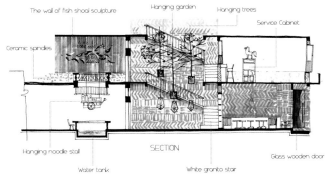

SECTION

First floor

1. Entrance
2. Inside
3. Outsie
4. Toilet
5. Reception- Bar
6. Dumbwaiter
7. Cascades
8. Private

Ground floor

AN'GARDEN CAFÉ

Area: **750 m²**
Location: **Ha Noi, Vietnam**

An'garden Café did not pursue a safe plan as other cafes did. Instead, this building aimed for an exclusive place that brings guests enjoyment from both coffee fragrance and picturesque surroundings. The facade of this shop intermingle large pieces of glass with steel frames. Random as the placement may be, it is still decorative and harmonious. Simple cement walls separate the pavement from indoor space. In order to minimize heavy feelings of cement, plants are considered an optimal solution that synchronizes with indoor environment.

Green elements along the space is another emphasis. Inside An'garden Café is the forgotten Hanging Gardens of Babylon which is partly replicated now. Climbers and coffee scent send you to another place other than busy and noisy Ha Noi. An'garden Café has two floors with a mezzanine that is suitable for those who want to focus on their work or come up with brilliant ideas. Yellow lighting, green layers and brick walls make this area attractive.

Design Agency: **Le House**
Photography: **Hyroyuki Oki**
Materials: **M&A Art Tiles—Handmade Ceramic and Brick Concrete, Hai Long Glass—Tempered Glass, Custom Metal Art, Rusted Steel**

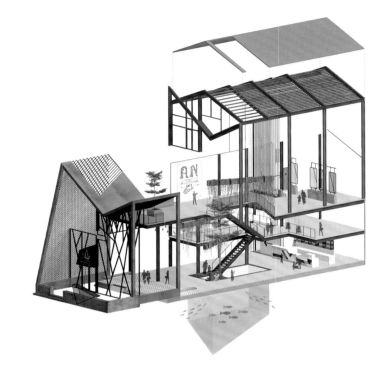

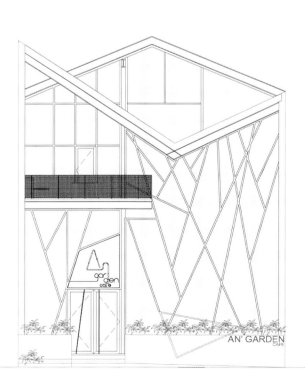

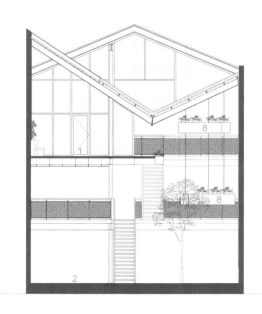

1. Outside
2. Inside
3. Lake
4. Reception
5. Kitchen
6. Toilet
7. Cascades
8. Hanging Tree
9. Children Playground

1 m   2 m   5 m

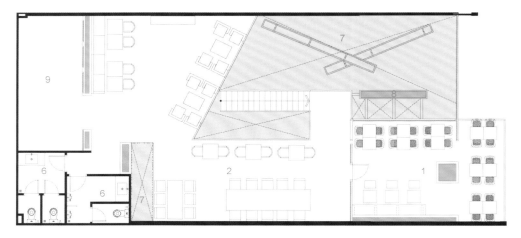

Second floor

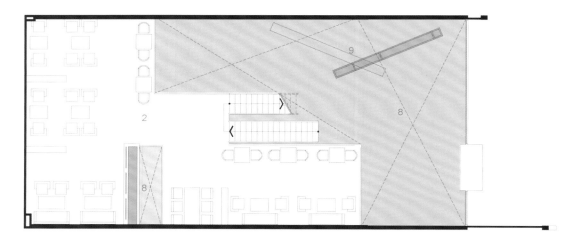

First floor

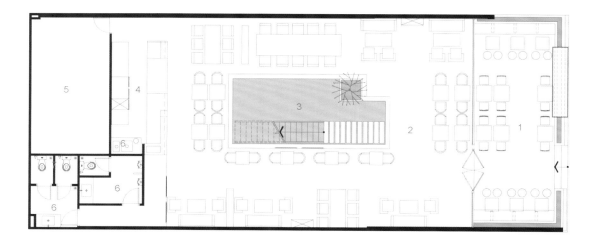

1. Outside
2. Inside
3. Lake
4. Reception
5. Kitchen
6. Toilet
7. Cascades
8. Hanging Tree
9. Children Playground

2 m
1 m   5 m

Ground floor

UU DAM
VEGETARIAN
RESTAURANT

Area: **1000 m²**
Location: **Hanoi, Vietnam**

Located in the heart of a crowded Hanoi Street, Uu Dam Vegetarian Restaurant quietly blossoms as a verdant and peaceful oasis welcoming thirsty pedestrians on the desert. Walking through the terrace, passing the Multi-face Buddha relief sculpture, visitors merge themselves into Uu Dam's space to cast off all their burdens outside the gate.

The three-storey space of the restaurant represents to three Buddhist periods: the Past, the Present and the Future. Each storey will be an interesting discovery for visitor who himself will experience what are trying to be sent by the sincere heart through each interior design corner, each manually selected table napkin, chopsticks, bowl and each vegetables of the restaurant. In the current noisy and busy life, it's hard to be not engulfed in such peaceful space to be back to human's religious meditation ego.

Design Agency: **Le House**
Photography: **Hiroyuki Oki**
Materials: **M&A Art Tiles—Handmade Ceramic and Brick Concrete, Hai Long glass—Tempered Glass, Custom Metal Art, Rusted Steel Material with "UU DAM" Board and Steel Statue of Buddha**

First floor

1. Entrance
2. Grasses & Tree zone
3. Siting Area inside
4. Toilet
5. Kitchen
6. Lobby
7. Reception- Bar
8. Dumbwaiter
9. Siting Area outside
10. Storage
11. Cascades

Ground floor

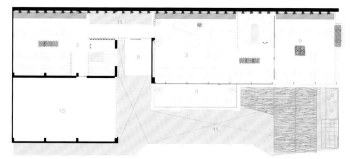

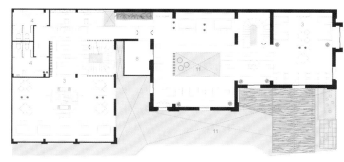

1. Entrance
2. Grasses & Tree zone
3. Siting Area inside
4. Toilet
5. Kitchen
6. Lobby
7. Reception- Bar
8. Dumbwaiter
9. Siting Area outside
10. Storage
11. Cascades

Second floor

INDEX

Alexander &CO.

Architects EAT

Architecture bureau DA

balbek bureau

Beleco

Biasol

biasol.com.au

Biasol is an award-winning Melbourne based design studio servicing the residential, hospitality, workplace and commercial markets on a local and global scale. They focus on interior design, building design, product design and branding to deliver projects with impact.

P010-021, P024-027

concrete

www.concreteamsterdam.nl

Since 1997 concrete develops concepts in architecture, interior design, urban development and brand development. concrete work with a team of 50 multidisciplinary creatives for corporations and institutions. Next to URBY, projects include citizenM hotels worldwide, W Hotels in London and Verbier, Zoku Lofts, Mongkok Skypark, Castell D'emporda, Supperclub worldwide, Rituals stores worldwide and they are currently working on W Hotel in Mumbai, Virgin Cruises, W Hotel in Osaka, Andaz Munchen and more.

P054-059, P088-089

DDDBrand

www.dddbrand.com

DDDBrand Design founded in 2008, and already served catering + entertainment brands for more than 10 years. DDDBrand focus on business positioning, brand culture designing, chain operation and construction designing and interior module designing.

P068-071

DesignAgency

www.thedesignagency.ca

DesignAgency is an internationally acclaimed design firm with studios in Toronto, Los Angeles, and Barcelona. Founded in Toronto in 1998 by partners Allen Chan, Matt Davis and Anwar Mekhayech, the full-service studio specializes in interior design and strategic brand creation, as well as architectural concepting, bespoke furniture and lighting, and visual communication. The team has an extensive knowledge of the hospitality sector ranging from Generator, the first design-led low-cost hotel brand, to luxury and lifestyle brands such as the Broadview Hotel, The St. Regis, and the Ritz Carlton Hotels in Toronto, The Dalmar in Fort Lauderdale (a Tribute hotel), and most recently, working with Hilton on the launch of "Motto by Hilton".

P090-093

DTZW Studio

www.dtzwstudio.com

DTZW Studio is a composite design company, was established by Li Xibin and Yao Ye in 2009. The studio is mainly engaged in brand building, product design, and architectural space design work, and they advocate the use of multielement, composite design methods for artistic and commercial creation.

P042-045

Fang Guoxi

fancyid.com

Fang Guoxi is the founder of Xiamen Fancy Design & Decoration Co., Ltd. He is also Vice General Manager and Design Director of Xiamen Huihuang Decoration Engineering Co., Ltd.

P170-173

FON STUDIO

www.fon-studio.com

FON STUDIO, a Beijing-Based indie studio, was co-founded by 3 old friends with sincere respects towards design aesthetics, as well as practice from spaces, products, visual arts and other perspectives. They hold the visceral conviction that the encounter between open experiment and rational analysis could generate awesome power. They always keep their curiosity alive, to create more projects with tactile appeal and temperature. Any cooperation proposal from congenial individuals or teams are welcomed. Looking forward to discovering more possibilities together.

P166-169

Francesc Rifé Studio

www.rife-design.com

Interior and industrial designer, Francesc Rifé (Sant Sadurní d'Anoia, 1969) founded his own studio in Barcelona in 1994. Influenced by minimalism and following a familiar tradition linked to craftsmanship, his work focuses on ways of approaching material honesty, spatial order and geometric proportion.

Currently, Francesc Rifé leads a team of professionals from several design fields. His projects, domestic and international, range from interior to industrial design, architecture, the creation of concepts, installations, graphics, and art direction. Throughout his career, Rifé has been awarded with prizes from the field of design such as Contract World, Red Dot, ICFF Editors, HiP in Chicago, FAD, and several ASCER awards.

P162-165

Golucci International Design

www.golucci.com

Golucci International Design was established by Taiwanese designer Lee Hsuheng in 2004. The highly motivated and qualified designers fully recognize the importance of professional acumen. Each project is conceptualized and developed by their experienced design team. Over the years, their works have included a wide range of Clubhouses, Hotels, Bars & Restaurants. Their approach to management ensures a high quality end product and they express the essence of their creative ideas to the best benefits of their clients.

P106-109, P114-125, P174-179

GONGSANGPLANET

www.gongsangplanet.com

GONGSANGPLANET started with the motto of "Share thinking, Imagine space" in 2009, Seoul.

A gongsang planet based on space design and brand design aims to research for new things and treat space as a special place to lead an increasingly popular culture. By consulting on all design elements in space, they have integrated design in each field, creating a highly complete image, providing a new level of design solution.

P072-077, P094-099

Hangzhou Trenchant Decoration Design co., LTD

www.tdxuanchi.com

Hangzhou Trenchant Decoration Design co., LTD. was established in 2010 and specialized in commercial space, public space, real estate space, visual art design. Provide commercial positioning, decoration design, lighting design, visual design, and other special services.

With "innovative design philosophy, strict design management, adapt to the design of the market" as the working principle, whether or not. The complete project is the perfect design to implement each project for the inspection standard, and for many years, the project has been higher. The level is active in the commercial design market, obtains the good reputation in the industry. Trenchant Design has cooperated with several international professional design companies, such as Shimao, Greentown, Transfar, Hangzhou metro, The starry city, starbucks catering management.Limited the company to achieve long-term strategic partnership.

P032-033

hcreates

www.hcreates.design

hcreates is an interior design studio based in Shanghai, designing projects across China and increasingly across Asia. hcreates works with like-minded clients to achieve spaces that are designed to enhance one's environment, and leave people feeling stimulated and inspired. Well known in Shanghai for creating contemporary restaurants and bars, hcreates continues to develop a significant portfolio of commercial and health and wellness spaces too.

Their design philosophy comes from an ingrained sense of Kiwi ingenuity, innovation and practicality. Design should be simple, clever and fun, creating spaces for people to collaborate and connect as they work, eat and play.

P190-195

House Fiction

www.housefiction.com

House Fiction is a down-to-earth design lab which based in Beijing. It was founded by architect Ji Yaqiong in 2017. They are experimenting in multi-discipline areas, and articulating their findings through art and commercial projects.

P038-041

Infinity Mind

www.infinitynide.com

Infinity Mind was founded in 2011. It takes "Free thinking" as its design philosophy, and yet it consciously persist in responsibility and obligation of exploring a new design philosophy. Been through many field surveys and in-depth practice, it attach great importance to material application and quality craftsmanship.

P126-129

Kimmel Eshkolot Architects

www.kimmel.co.il

Kimmel Eshkolot Architects is an Israeli architecture practice, founded in 1986 in Tel Aviv by Etan Kimmel and Michal Kimmel Eshkolot. In their first years of practice, they were involved in the preservation and rehabilitation of Tel Aviv's historical Neve Tzedek neighborhood. In 2011, they won the Rechter Prize for Architecture, considered to be the most prestigious award for architecture in Israel. They received the award for the design of a rehabilitation center in Be'er Sheva, in the south of Israel. This project was also selected for project of the year in the international competition of the magazine Israeli Architecture. The practice is currently involved in dozens of projects in different scales, both in Israel and in Europe.

P134-137

Le House

www.le-house.vn

Architect LE HUNG TRONG is the founder of Le House Company. Before of the establishment of Le House company in 2015, it took LE HUNG TRONG nearly 9 years for Archviz Artist position in an architecture firm when he graduated a valedictorian from Van Lang University—Architecture Design. In the next 7 years, he was alone on his way to look for the difference in design thinking. When he realized completely that he had enough confidence to start up his own company based on his passions and experiences. He decided to do it with those wishing to contribute Le House's creative and making the image of Vietnam architecture to international friends.

P218-232

Lukstudio

www.lukstudiodesign.com

Lukstudio is a boutique design practice based in Shanghai, China. Founded by Christina Luk in 2011, the studio is comprised of an international team with diverse backgrounds and cultural perspectives. With a common desire to challenge the status quo of the environment, the team finds joy in creating meaningful design solutions for others.

P050-051

Masquespacio

www.masquespacio.com

Masquespacio is an award winning creative consultancy created in 2010 by Ana Milena Hernández Palacios and Christophe Penasse. Combining the 2 disciplines of their founders, interior design and marketing, the Spanish design agency creates branding and interior projects through a unique approach that results in fresh and innovative concepts rewarded with a continued international recognition by media specialized in design, fashion and lifestyle trends. They have worked on projects in several countries like Norway, the USA, France, Portugal, Germany and Spain. Actually they are working on different hospitality projects in Spain and Germany.

P110-113

Megre Interiors

megreinteriors.com

Founded in 2008 by Yuna Megre, Megre Interiors is a Moscow based boutique design company specializing in hospitality design. With completed and current projects in Moscow, St. Petersburg, London, New York, Boston, Los Angeles, Leukerbad (Switzerland), Baku, Tbilisi, Dubai, amongst others, Megre Interiors is a company with an international outlook. Megre Interiors is a team of two dozen highly dedicated specialists—designers, architects, 3D artists, buyers, managers—who take a team based agile approach to delivering quality design & documentation in tight time frames. In 2018, Megre Interiors expanded to the United States and has opened a satellite office in Los Angeles where they have begun work in the hospitality sector.

P100-103, P138-141

New Practice Studio

newpractice.co

New Practice Studio is a New York and Shanghai based interdisciplinary collaboration between architects, interior designers, graphic designers and brand strategists. Their work explores possibilities in architecture, urbanism and visual communication as ways to transform the stereotypes of everyday experience into the prototypes of new space and idea. With services from urban planning, architecture design, interior design, furniture design, construction administration to graphic design and branding, they strive to fulfill their clients' ambition through comprehensive design perspective and rigorous attention to detail and execution.

P078-079

Pure's Design Studio

www.puresdesign.com

Pure's Design Studio is specialized in the interior, landscape, architecture, and photography. They are committed to providing customers with a full range of design solutions. Their goal is to explore the new ways to solve conflicts. Rather than simplifying the problem, they serve to use pluralistic ways to fulfill the needs of the growing metropolises, and they tap the tremendous power behind the seemingly problematic but vibrant urban architecture.

P046-049

Republican Metropolis Architecture

www.i-rma.hk

Republican Metropolis Architecture (RMA) has been committed to the spirit of innovation for the community to provide a variety of design products, creative, imaginative creativity design to drive more brand value, works cover construction, top CLUB, catering office, private homes, Innovative bold design for the space into the new vitality, during the works won a number of top global event awards.

P146-149

Sella Concept

www.sella-concept.com

Sella Concept is a design studio and business consultancy. Set up by Tatjana von Stein and Gayle Noonan, who met while creating and curating Clerkenwell London, the company specialises in shaping spaces that engage and inspire all who set foot in them. Thanks to a combination of Gayle's graphic design background and Tatjana's track record in retail and hospitality concept development, they are able to offer a full spectrum of design services to commercial clients, spanning interiors, visual identity and branding, event design and curation. So far, the duo has helped Google launch Pixel in London, Netflix make its debut in at the Cannes Film Festival and Instagram deliver its talks programme during London Fashion Week, alongside designing eye-catching and engaging retail spaces, restaurants, bars, hotels and members' clubs. Sella Concept has a knack for making spaces that both meet business goals and surpass consumer expectations.

P022-023

Studio Formafatal

www.formafatal.cz

Studio Formafatal was founded by architect Dagmar Štěpánová, and the team is now Dagmar, Jan, Martina, Katarína, Iveta, Dana, Michael and Daniela. They create public spaces, where people feel like home, and homes, that are tailored to the clients needs. All projects they approach individually and with focus on specific human needs. Individual approach for each project is based on mutual understanding with the client, enthusiasm, natural collaboration and unified conceptual solutions. They solve projects complexly from creative concept to realization, with attention to detail.

P028-031

Studio Roslyn

studioroslyn.com

Studio Roslyn is an interior design studio based in Vancouver, British Columbia. It specializes in developing design solutions for the built environments that are integral to the success of client's businesses. Put simply, designers from Studio Roslyn believe that creativity is not in conflict with commerce. Their work crosses the boundaries between art and design, fashion, and architecture—while keeping a sense of vivacity throughout.

P060-061

Studio UNLTD

www.studiounltd.com

Founded in 2009 by Greg Bleier, Los Angeles based Studio UNLTD is an award-winning design firm equally adept at the varied disciplines of interior architecture, furniture and lighting. STUDIO UNLTD is a small and agile team of 9 people whose primary focus is hospitality projects with a specialization in restaurant design. The success is driven by their ability to transform client vision, brand and functionality into thoughtfully crafted reality. They love working with passionate people; whether it be clients, artisans, world class chefs, barmen, or tastemakers.

Tsutsumi & Associates

www.tsuaa.jp

Tsutsumi & Associates was established by Yoshimasa Tsutsumi in 2009. He was born in Fukuoka in 1978, graduated from the University of Tokyo in 2003. The main awards which he received are JCD Design Award GOLD prize, SILVER prize, Ryue Nishizawa prize, DFA silver award, APIDA bronze award, A+D china award BEST of category, etc.

Weng Shanwei

www.wengshanwei.com

Based in Hangzhou and Shanghai of China, Weng Shanwei focuses on the field of spatial design. On the basis of individual perception and boundaries, he strives to explore and respond to a possible fresh connection, inclusion and association, or even a conflict between space, objects and art. Trained in fashion design, Weng Shanwei has been engaged in graphic design for more than 10 years since his graduation from university. In 2011, he established AN

Design with a team dedicated to interior and architectural design. He is also engaged in art practice and has created the following works: "Capture Edge", "Get Hot Water" (image), behavioral device text "Diameter 29 Kilometers" and image project "Copy Summer". Meanwhile, he actively participated in international and domestic lectures, reviews, competitions, exhibitions and exchanges in various forms, and has won several awards from international design competitions and media selection.

YOD Design Lab

yoddesign.com.ua

YOD Design Lab is an active participant in the Ukrainian market of design services since 2004. It is a cohesive team of designers, architects, designers and project managers. Studio numbers more than 100 successfully completed projects in Ukraine, including several projects implemented abroad: in Astana and Almaty (Kazakhstan), Bucharest (Romania), Moscow (Russia), Budapest (Hungary), Riyadh (Saudi Arabia).

ACKNOWLEDGEMENTS

We would like to thank all of the artists involved for granting us permission to publish their works, as well as the photographers who have generously allowed us to use their images. We are also very grateful to many other people whose names do not appear in the credits but who made specific contributions and provided support. Without these people, we would not have been able to share these beautiful works with readers around the world.